Simple Steps to Data Encryption

Simple Steps to Data Encryption
A Practical Guide to Secure Computing

Peter Loshin

ELSEVIER

AMSTERDAM • BOSTON • HEIDELBERG • LONDON
NEW YORK • OXFORD • PARIS • SAN DIEGO
SAN FRANCISCO • SINGAPORE • SYDNEY • TOKYO
Syngress is an imprint of Elsevier

SYNGRESS.

Acquiring Editor: Steve Elliot
Development Editor: Benjamin Rearick
Project Manager: Mohana Natarajan

Syngress is an imprint of Elsevier
225 Wyman Street, Waltham, MA 02451, USA

First published 2013

Notices
Knowledge and best practice in this field are constantly changing. As new research and experience broaden our understanding, changes in research methods, professional practices, or medical treatment may become necessary.

Practitioners and researchers must always rely on their own experience and knowledge in evaluating and using any information, methods, compounds, or experiments described herein. In using such information or methods they should be mindful of their own safety and the safety of others, including parties for whom they have a professional responsibility.

To the fullest extent of the law, neither the Publisher nor the authors, contributors, or editors, assume any liability for any injury and/or damage to persons or property as a matter of products liability, negligence or otherwise, or from any use or operation of any methods, products, instructions, or ideas contained in the material herein.

British Library Cataloguing in Publication Data
A catalogue record for this book is available from the British Library

Library of Congress Cataloging-in-Publication Data
A catalog record for this book is available from the Library of Congress

ISBN: 978-0-12-411483-8

For information on all Syngress publications
visit our website at www.syngress.com

This book has been manufactured using Print On Demand technology. Each copy is produced to order and is limited to black ink. The online version of this book will show color figures where appropriate.

Working together
to grow libraries in
developing countries

www.elsevier.com • www.bookaid.org

CONTENTS

TO THE READER

Did you pick this book up just to figure out how to encrypt a file or validate a download? Then this page is for you; if not, it's my promise to provide useful information on the first page and every page after that. These tips are for users with Gnu Privacy Guard (GnuPG) already installed--which includes all major Linux distributions[1]. GnuPG works at the command line, so OS X and Linux users open a terminal window, Windows users open the command line window.

To encrypt a file (example.doc) with a secret passphrase, use this command:

```
$ gpg --symmetric example.doc[2]
```

You'll be prompted for a passphrase, twice (to confirm it) and then a file will be written called example.doc.gpg (WARNING: the original file is still there, in plaintext!). The encrypted file can be decrypted back (as example.doc) with this command (plus the passphrase, when prompted[3]):

```
$ gpg --output example.doc --decrypt example.doc.gpg
```

The recipient will be prompted to enter the passphrase to decrypt the file.

To verify a digitally signed file, such as when downloading a piece of software from the Internet, given the download file named example.doc and a signature file named example.doc.sig both in the current directory, use this command:

```
$ gpg --verify example.doc.sig example.doc
```

---

[1]For Windows, install Gpg4win (gpg4win.org). For Mac OS X, install GPGTools (gpgtools.org). See the Gnu Privacy Guard site (gnupg.org) for other options.

[2]The monospace font and the $ character indicate this is an example of a command being entered at the command line. The $ indicates the system is ready to accept a command; the command is typed in and after you type it you press the Enter key to make something happen.

[3]If you decrypt right after encrypting it, you may not be prompted for a passphrase, as your computer "remembers" it; see section "Pinentry Dialog Box and RAM Caching" of Chapter 4, for more about this issue.

If the file verifies, the resulting message will include the words "Good signature," among much more information (which may include a warning that the signing key is not certified--don't worry about this, for now). If not, "Good signature" will *not* appear (other information will be displayed, depending on what happened).

Good luck--and if you want to know more about how this works, keep reading!

What Is This?

This book is about learning to protect data with encryption. It's a combination primer, story, guide, and handbook on how to use Gnu Privacy Guard (GnuPG) encryption software to protect *data in motion* (messages or files being sent over the Internet), followed by a brief discussion of how to protect *data at rest* by using full disk encryption (FDE) on modern operating systems (OSes).

You will learn to use cryptography in a practical way: to encrypt and to decrypt a message or file, to validate a digitally signed message or file, to manage encryption keys, and to work securely with encryption tools.

That means how and why to do it, but not how it works. If you are interested in the science and engineering aspects of how cryptography works--algorithms, acronyms, standards, and specifications--there are many good resources for learning about those topics online[1]. Online is also where you'll find the best information about installing encryption software, because online is where it's most likely to be up-to-date.

The objective here is to get started doing encryption, not to know why it works or where it came from. However, just for the record--and to make sure we're on the same page--here is a brief summary of what cryptography is and what it can do.

WHAT IS CRYPTOGRAPHY?

Cryptography is the science/practice of "writing in secret" ("crypto" = "secret," "graphy" = "writing"). Cryptographic functions are generally defined as algorithms or protocols, rules that govern how data is processed to turn *plaintext* (unencrypted data) into *ciphertext* (encrypted data).

---

[1] *Fundamentals of Cryptography* (http://crypto.loshin.com/2012/11/20/fundamentals-of-cryptography/) has links to some good introductory cryptography articles.

WHAT CAN CRYPTOGRAPHY DO?

Encryption is what most people think about when they think about cryptography: taking *plaintext* and turning it into what looks like gibberish, a.k.a. *ciphertext*.

Done right, encryption protects private data by making it difficult (in some cases almost impossible) for an attacker to uncover plaintext. Depending on circumstances--such as whether the user creates a strong passphrase[2] or whether the user is careful about leaving information vulnerable on their computer--it may be next to impossible--or trivially easy--for an attack to succeed, depending on a user's choices.

The goal of using encryption is to make it harder for others to uncover our secrets. The idea is that whatever amount of expertise and computer time is needed to break our encryption should cost more than the perceived value of the information being decrypted.

BASIC CRYPTOGRAPHIC FUNCTIONS

Modern cryptography depends on three types of functions:

Single-key or *symmetric* encryption algorithms use one ("single") key for both encryption and decryption. "Symmetric" means the encryption and decryption processes are reverses of each other. I must share the secret passphrase with anyone I want to be able to decrypt my encrypted data.

Public key or *asymmetric* encryption algorithms use a pair of keys: the public key and the private key. "Asymmetric" means that the process of encryption with the public key can only be reversed (decrypted) by using the private key (and vice versa). If you want to send me an encrypted message, you must have my public key--and only someone who has access to my private key (presumably, just me) can decrypt messages encrypted with my public key.

Hash functions accept plaintext data of any length and produce a fixed-length *hash*. These functions are sometimes called *message digests* or *one-way encryption functions*; the fixed-length hashes they produce appear to be random data. When correctly implemented, the hash value serves as a kind of digital fingerprint and can be

---

[2]*Passphrase* and not *password*; passphrase implies longer and more complicated. See http://crypto. loshin.com/2013/01/17/passphrases-vs-passwords/ for more.

used to verify that data received has not been modified in transit: the slightest change to the plaintext produces a completely different hash result.

Cryptographic processes combine some or all of these functions in various ways for different results. For example, secure web sites store hashes of passphrases--not the passphrases themselves. When you create a passphrase, the web site hashes it and saves the hash value. Every time you log in, the web site hashes your passphrase and compares the result to the hash value stored in the database. Wrong passphrase => wrong hash, user not authenticated. Correct passphrase => correct hash, user authenticated. Even if an attacker breaks into the web site database, he can't recover your passphrase.

Likewise, public key encryption software combines public key and single-key encryption: the actual data is encrypted with single-key encryption, and only the encryption key is actually public key encrypted. This saves time: public key encryption takes more computer cycles and thus a long file might take minutes or even hours to public key encrypt--especially troublesome if the same data must be encrypted for more than one recipient (more than one public key).

DOES "SECRET" MEAN THE SAME AS "PRIVATE"?

A *secret key* and a *private key* are both meant to be "secrets" in the sense that I don't tell them to anyone[3]. My *private key*, though, is for me only. It's private! No sharing at all, or I've lost control over my public key pair, and that means two things follow: first, I can no longer assert that anything digitally signed with my private key actually originated from me (my digital signature can't be trusted anymore), and second, whoever has my private key can now read any messages encrypted to my public key (all data encrypted with that key is no longer secure).

A *public key pair* consists of a *public key* (the opposite of secret/private since it is meant to be published), and a private key ("secret" in that it's a key meant to be kept secret by its owner). That's for public

---

[3]That is, except when I use a *secret key* to do symmetric (single-key) encryption and want to share the encrypted data with someone else. Then, I *have* to share the secret with the person I'm communicating with.

key encryption, a.k.a. *asymmetric encryption*, a.k.a. *two-key encryption*: private keys and public keys, in pairs.

The confusion sneaks in when discussing symmetric encryption, a.k.a. *single-key, shared-key*, or *one-key* encryption[4]; what some writers call a *secret* key may refer to the private half of a public key pair (*private* key), and what they call a *private* key sometimes refers to a secret key used for symmetric encryption.

It should go without saying that I will be using these terms unambiguously and urge others to do the same: *private* implies public key; *secret* implies a single key.

What Else Do I Need?

To get started doing encryption requires relatively little:

> *a modern computer* (desktop, notebook, or netbook should all work) running an OS on which GnuPG will run (which is most of them),
> *an Internet connection* (highly recommended, though not technically mandatory),
> a strong interest or compelling reason to use encryption.

The right motivation--the reason you want to learn to do encryption--is critical. There's not much point in learning to do cryptography if you have no reason to do it other than because it's interesting or cool, but a good reason is a great motivator as well as a great incentive for doing cryptography correctly. A "good reason" is any reason that motivates you--and your motivation is entirely your own business.

WHAT OS SHOULD I USE?

To start, use whatever computer and OS you like best--or whatever you're stuck with. There are versions of GnuPG that run on your OS, and working on your preferred/usual OS will help make it easier to get started.

---

[4]Some writers, unfortunately including many people who are considered experts, use the term *private key* to describe the secret key used in symmetric encryption, or the term *secret key* to describe the private key of a public key pair. This can be quite confusing, but GnuPG is most often used for public key cryptography, so assuming that private = secret can minimize confusion.

Once you become comfortable using GnuPG, however, consider investing some time in learning to use it on a good Linux distribution: most GnuPG activity and development is done on Linux, and it is easier to use GnuPG on Linux than on commercial OSes. Most modern Linux distributions include GnuPG, so there is no need to install any software, and most Linux distributions can be *live booted* which means they can be booted from a DVD/CD or thumb drive, allowing you to use Linux on almost any system without installing anything.

HOW DO I DO ALL THIS STUFF?

Just because this is a book, we don't have to pretend the Internet doesn't exist.

If you have any questions about how to do things described here, answers are usually a few keystrokes away at your favorite search engine. Though I could have filled up hundreds of pages with instructions on how and why to use Linux, how to burn a live-boot DVD, how to use a text editor, or the history of open source software--*in a book about doing cryptography*--I thought it would be better to focus on using GnuPG to do cryptography.

INTRODUCTION

When I buy a computer book, I'm impatient. I want to get to the part of the book that tells me everything I need to get my stuff done. For this book, the important information is how to encrypt, decrypt, and digitally sign your data. That's why the first page explains how to encrypt a file and how to verify a digital signature: *Actionable information on every page* is my motto.

There is much you should know about how to use encryption safely and securely, but it's not easy to present all that information comprehensively and exhaustively but also accessibly (that is, "won't put the reader to sleep by page 17").

I began writing this book using the industry standard for computer books: start with the history of encryption, followed by a history of encryption software, then a comprehensive list of all current encryption software and exhaustive installation instructions on all platforms, and then the systematic death march defining and describing every step of every command and option of every program.

That was so boring that *I* couldn't *write* for more than 20 minutes at a time before nodding off, let alone read it. Rather than attempting yet another catalog of mostly useless and mind-numbing technical trivia, I decided it would be more interesting (for all of us) to tell a story about how someone learns to do encryption.

Thus, what you are reading is a work of fiction: the characters and situations are made up, intended to give a human face to how encryption works and is used. The stuff about Bob and Sam, those things are made up--but what those people do with their computers is all real and true.

I could have included more introductory material, explained more about why open source software is preferable for security functions, why the command line beats GUI interfaces for learning about encryption, even how to use the command line. I have included notes to help you get started working along with the text, but most of what you need is revealed as the story moves forward. All in good time and (hopefully) never so much as to become boring.

If you just want the exhaustive set of facts and instructions, without context, pick a Gnu Privacy Guard tutorial[1] and have at it. If you want to understand and use encryption in the real world, read on and enjoy!

---

[1]See http://crypto.loshin.com/2012/11/17/gnupg-tutorials/ for some good ones.

CHAPTER 1

Using Gnu Privacy Guard

Bob lives in Sylvania, a tiny nation ruled by a dictator who forbids all printed dissent and criticism. However, emboldened on a visit to the United States, Bob wrote his own brief editorial, on a cocktail napkin while sitting at the airport bar, waiting to board his plane home. It begins:

Free Sylvania!

Those two words alone could send Bob to the Sylvanian gulag if discovered back home. As the exhilaration of creation wears off, Bob downloads and installs Gnu Privacy Guard[1] to encrypt his work. He's been told it's good for encryption, and it's free, so why not?

Bob's plane leaves Logan in 15 minutes, and when he starts reading the tutorial for GnuPG, he panics: it goes on at great length about *public key encryption* and *key pairs* and *generating key pairs* and generating *revocation certificates*, and even when he gets to the part about encrypting a file, it says he'll need *someone else's* public key to encrypt *to*. Bob quietly starts to freak out.

Fortunately for Bob, he's sitting next to a man who picks up on Bob's anxiety and offers to help. This good Samaritan is actually named Sam, and he just happens to know all about GnuPG. After they introduce themselves, Sam says, "Listen Bob, I can help you get it all sorted out, don't worry. We've even got time for a drink before they board your flight."

1.1 KEEPING DATA SECRET, FOR A NOVICE GnuPG USER

After seating themselves in the lounge, Sam says, "You're in a hurry and need to encrypt a file. You've just installed GnuPG but don't know much about encryption, so your best bet is to use single-key encryption with a strong passphrase. It's easy: all you need is GnuPG, no need to set anything up."

---

[1] Go to www.gnupg.org/download for the official downloads; http://gpg4win.org/ for GnuPG for Windows and https://www.gpgtools.org/ for GPGTools (OS X).

Sam explains, "Using symmetric (secret) key encryption I can make sure no one can see the contents but me (and whoever I share the passphrase with). That's how I'd do it if I was in a hurry and didn't have time to study tutorials or books."

Bob looks pointedly at his watch, then the departure board, but Sam continues, "Symmetric encryption is easy with GnuPG because I don't need to generate my own public key pair *or* get anyone else's key: I just enter an encryption command and enter a strong passphrase for my encrypted file. Are you ready?"

1.2 THE SIMPLEST EXAMPLE: GnuPG SYMMETRIC ENCRYPTING TEXT

Sam opens his laptop and a terminal window, and explains to Bob: "I think of GnuPG commands as if they're sentences; every GnuPG sentence starts with 'gpg', and there are grammar rules in this sentence like 'options first, then files' and 'options before commands'. You have to be careful to follow the grammar, but it's usually easy. Here's how I encrypt a file called example.txt[2]," and he types:

```
$ gpg -c exampel.txt
gpg: can't open 'exampel.txt': No such file or directory
gpg: symmetric encryption of 'exampel.txt' failed: No such file or directory
$
```

"Oh crud, what the..." Sam, reading the GnuPG error messages onscreen after he hit <Enter>, realizes he misspelled the filename. "Oops, that's what you get when the filename doesn't exist in the current directory; it happens all the time and isn't a big deal. And if you get an error message that doesn't make sense, you can usually get help by searching for that message on your favorite web search engine." Sam retypes the command and is prompted for a passphrase[3] (twice):

```
$ gpg -c example.txt
$
```

---

[2]Files in these examples will always be read from or written to the current working directory in the terminal/console session (unless otherwise specified).

[3]Depending on the OS, you'll get a different kind of prompt; usually it's in a small GUI window that pops up specifically for secure passphrase entry.

"OK, I entered a passphrase, but now, nothing. Or is it?" Sam says as he shows Bob a directory listing[4] that includes a new file called example.txt.gpg. "When GnuPG creates new files, it names them by adding the .gpg extension."

Sam continued: "Here's my thinking when I enter that command. First, gpg = 'run GnuPG'. Then, -c, an abbreviation for the command --symmetric, for single-key encryption. If I used the -e option (--encrypt) that would be for doing public key encryption; I'll show you public key encryption later, if you like." Sam sipped his drink.

"So that's my command: 'GnuPG, encrypt something!'. 'Something' is whatever comes after the command, in this case a file called example.txt in the current directory[5]. I hit <Enter> and I'm prompted to enter a passphrase, and it should be something hard to crack. Good passphrases are hard to come up with, but they should be longer than 8−10 characters at the very least, and should appear as random as possible, including upper and lower case letters, symbols and numbers. It will be hard to remember, but it will also be hard for someone to guess. Just remember that if you forget it, *you* won't be able to decrypt your file either."

Bob asks, "How *do* I decrypt this file? Do I need GnuPG to decrypt?"

1.3 DECRYPTING A FILE (SYMMETRIC KEY)

Sam said: "It's easy to decrypt a file, but you do need GnuPG (or compatible software[6]) to do it. Here's how," Sam says as he types the command and hits <Enter>, entering a passphrase when prompted:

```
$ gpg example.txt.gpg
gpg: CAST5 encrypted data
gpg: encrypted with 1 passphrase
gpg: WARNING: message was not integrity protected
$
```

---

[4]dir on Windows, ls on Mac OS X or Linux.
[5]A *directory* is the text-only version of a folder; folder is the icon for the directory.
[6]Any program that supports the OpenPGP standard for encryption should work. OpenPGP is discussed later in the chapter.

"Sam, what does that WARNING mean?" Bob asks. "Oh, don't worry about that: GnupG can be a chatty little program, and not always completely clear. The first two lines mean the file was encrypted with the CAST5 algorithm--the default for GnuPG single-key encryption, with one passphrase. The last line means the file wasn't digitally signed."

Sam continues: "The messages tell you the file was encrypted successfully. GnuPG stored the decrypted file, named example.txt, to disk; now both files are in my directory. I didn't have to explicitly say I'm decrypting (though I could have used the --decrypt option for clarity). Often you can just enter gpg <file_name> and GnuPG 'does the right thing' with the file--if it's GnuPG compatible[7], like if it's an encrypted file and you enter a valid passphrase. If you enter a file that's not GnuPG compatible, you'll get an error, GnuPG won't assume you want to encrypt unless you tell it explicitly, with -c for symmetric encryption, or -e for public key."

Bob spoke up: "Hang on, Sam, do I *have* to save it to a file? I'm not sure I want to save my secrets as plaintext on my hard drive."

Sam answers, "That's a good point. You'd probably rather just use the --decrypt or -d command, because GnuPG sends its output directly to the *standard output* (that's a fancy name for the terminal window, or console)." He types a few lines, and says, "here's what it looks like, I'm really just telling the computer: 'run GnuPG and decrypt (some file)' ":

```
$ gpg --decrypt foo.bar.gpg
gpg: CAST5 encrypted data
gpg: encrypted with 1 passphrase
the name of this file is foo.bar
this is a simple 3-line file
this is the third line
gpg: WARNING: message was not integrity protected
$
```

Sam went on: "After I enter the passphrase, GnuPG prints the decrypted file out to the console--it's highlighted here, a 3-line text file. This is a simple way to decrypt files with GnuPG: just enter gpg -d <filename> (whatever the filename actually is); if the file can be

---

[7]GnuPG creates files that conform to the OpenPGP format. Any programmer that knows the format can (theoretically) write a program to recognize and work with GnuPG files.

decrypted GnuPG just splashes it out to the screen, no worries about having incriminating evidence saved on your disk, either."

As Bob peers at the screen, Sam goes on: "Bob, you should know that when I have a plaintext file and I encrypt it, GnuPG creates a new file for the encrypted version (that's what we call *ciphertext*) but *nothing happens to the original plaintext file*. It's still sitting there, so you should securely erase[8] the plaintext file, not just delete it, if you're worried about someone finding it. Otherwise it could get you in trouble."

Bob says, "But I'd rather not save a dangerous secret on my disk at all, ever; even if I delete it, it can still be recovered--can't it?" Sam answers, "Yes, it often can be recovered, but there are ways to make it harder..." when Bob interrupts: "Is there any way I can encrypt something without saving plaintext to the disk at all?"

As the flight attendant announces "All passengers attention. Now please board Sylvania Air Flight 789," over the intercom, the men finish their drinks and start packing up. "Listen Bob," Sam says, "here's my card: give me a call if you want to talk more about this. I'll be in Sylvania for a couple of weeks on business, so let's meet for another drink and I'll answer all your encryption questions then."

Bob examines the card: "Sam Mallory, Consultant", a phone number, an email address (`sam.mallory.404@gmail.com`) and a string of what seems to be nonsense letters and numbers; then looks up to see Sam lining up for Bob's own flight. Bob hurries after Sam; he wants an answer to his last question before their paths diverge.

1.4 ENCRYPTING INTERACTIVELY

"Hey, Sam--looks like we're on the same flight! Where are you sitting?" Bob asks as he catches up to Sam. "Please, can you explain how to encrypt interactively?"

Sam, ignoring Bob's first question, replies, "Sure, interactive encrypting. It's not hard, just a bit strange for people who are used to working in a GUI all the time."

---

[8]For more about secure deletion, see EFF "Secure Deletion (Surveillance Self-Defense project)" at https://ssd.eff.org/tech/deletion.

Sam clears his throat. "Remember how the GnuPG command looked? First it said `gpg`, then it said what to do, like `--encrypt`, and then we typed in a filename to encrypt. I said if you leave off the command but give a filename, GnuPG can figure out what to do with the file if it's an OpenPGP-compliant file." Bob nods as the line inches forward.

Sam says, "The last part of the command, where you put the thing you want to encrypt or decrypt or digitally sign is (often) optional. If you leave that part blank, GnuPG assumes that you've got something to enter interactively. Instead of doing anything after you hit <Enter>, GnuPG will wait for you to enter something to encrypt or decrypt."

Bob thinks about it for a moment as the line inches forward and asks, "How does that work, though? What gets output? How do you enter something to encrypt?"

"Good questions," says Sam. "This is where it gets a little more complicated, because you have to use an option, in this case the `--armor` or `-a` option. 'Armor' is short for 'ASCII-armored'."

"Huh? What does that mean?" Bob goggles as Sam inches forward in line.

1.5 ASCII ARMOR

Bob catches up as Sam says: "You want your ciphertext to look as random as possible. That means random bits, which when you try to print it out as text it looks like crazy gibberish, lots of weird symbols. It looks like your computer's barfing at the command line." Sam opens his laptop to demonstrate. "Like this":[9]

```
$ cat example.txt.gpg
?^??wj???6?1w?t?6 ???'?[?x        #??n?J??W??g*Ez!I5A7H@?
/;??'???<?vɐ`□??K
)????????.?C?ʊ                                    ????□H?<
?'??f????z5????p~??2j08?~?g?)?^!?ᵣe??!n?c?=□??/x?p*0?>dV"
+[??헤V?!훼?{??x??|[?M}/
            ??$??F+??Uj?y????|`lj?z???kL?r.
$
```

---

[9]Sam uses the UNIX/Linux/OS X command `cat`, for "reading files sequentially, writing them to the standard output." In Windows, use the command `more filename.txt` to list the file `filename.txt`.

"That's called *binary output*. Computers can read it, but people can't make sense of it, at all." Bob nods, and Sam continues:

"Sometimes we want GnuPG to produce encrypted output that uses letters and numbers that humans can accurately decode--something we can print out to the terminal window or stick in an email message. It looks like letters and numbers, but it's *random-looking* letters and numbers that don't seem to mean anything."

"*ASCII armor* is a way to get that kind of human-readable output; it means, 'encrypt this data but output only standard alphanumeric characters'. It makes more sense when you can look at it." Sam types a bit more and shows Bob an ASCII-armored file:

```
-----BEGIN PGP MESSAGE-----

jA0EAwMCAhOLCBblqDyrye1J/xOQtWF4UDri7fzpeD9xY8TtPVsQDwliwPh4m1Aw
68MCsFNK9chXGncdiZq+fd7f9tIdLAXXb2nLJip3JUp05z/HjjGSvKQ5LnRdD3H7
OmWDxNwpq99dSsxKwB5AoC/zlkW4XFR644/e0yn06PUflwZnYldx6UivxbEhtKeL
t5ZIvwCfuHma7C+Ye1Y2q3ZkfLGI0IEVfM40Ypzmr15LMCpLISN0E3OCJsyKfveR
[and so on, you get the idea...]
```

Sam tucks his laptop under his arm as the flight attendant takes his boarding pass and ushers him toward the plane; Sam turns to Bob and says, "Maybe I can show you more on the plane. See you later!" and walks off--as the other attendant turns to Bob and, looking at his boarding pass, says, "Sir, we've overbooked this flight today, would you please wait a moment?"

Accustomed to long lines and dodgy supply back home in Sylvania, Bob waits, outwardly placid and smiling neutrally--and is rewarded almost immediately as the flight attendant looks up from his terminal to say, "Mr. Wobble, we have a seat in first class for you today, would that be acceptable?" Without waiting for an answer, the attendant ushers Bob toward the front of the plane and seats him next to his new friend, in the nearly empty first-class compartment.

"Oh, hey, congratulations! Coach on this flight is always a sardine tin. Get comfortable and I'll show you interactive encryption and ASCII armoring," says Sam as he opens his laptop again. "Look:"

```
$ gpg -ac
```

"I've just started GnuPG with the option, -a, to generate output in ASCII armor, and a command, -c, to do symmetric encryption.

Notice I don't have to give each option its own hyphen--but I could, if I wanted[10]."

"Since I haven't specified an input file, GnuPG gives me a completely empty line, and I can start typing my message. When I'm done, I have to enter an 'end-of-file' sequence)[11]. GnuPG prompts for a passphrase (twice); here's the result:"

```
$ gpg -ac
This is just a silly little message, that's going to be completely secret
-----BEGIN PGP MESSAGE-----

jA0EAwMCK133JIYA9SOryVxTRYapN5zzOUg5YnDjlVl5ncEiB2oxmFzCtXiulgm3
Xodix78mScGA0t+GWkugeMbPo5h+ROQ6TvmgIqnTWtS5HdoWH54tAb8OLKmqmGdX
SBVLONJrFMD1NuFzFw==
=GBG6
-----END PGP MESSAGE-----
```

Sam says: "The plaintext is that line of text I typed in after the command; the ciphertext output is under that line. See the lines with hyphens that say BEGIN PGP MESSAGE and END PGP MESSAGE? Those are the part of the ASCII armor that shows where ciphertext begins and ends."

Bob, staring at the lines, asks "What is this 'PGP'? Is it part of GnuPG?"

Sam says, "It's a long story. 'PGP' stands for 'Pretty Good Privacy', the first real end user encryption software, written by Philip Zimmermann back in 1991. It was a big deal because the US government considered strong encryption munitions, so it was illegal to 'export'. With software, that just means downloading it over the Internet, and Zimmerman could have gone to federal prison for it. He stuck his neck out, and he's a hero to many. It eventually got sorted out, but with the genie out of the bottle the feds backed down and now almost everyone has, or can get, strong encryption[12]. If it weren't

---

[10] *Sometimes* is the operative word; other times, you've got to keep options separate.

[11] On Windows: press <Enter> then <ctrl-z> then <Enter>. On OS X/Linux, press <Enter> then <ctrl-d>. That is, the <Control> key plus the letter "z" (or "d"). Pressing <ctrl-c> ("abort") quits GnuPG without executing any command.

[12] Encryption software can be difficult to come by in some countries where Internet access and access to computers may be limited by the government.

for Zimmermann, we might not be sitting here talking about encryption."

As the flight attendant serves Bob and Sam flutes of champagne and moist warm towels, Sam continues: "PGP fascinated Internet pioneers back then, and as the only practical, accessible, program for encryption, PGP was eventually written into Internet standards, and used widely enough that an Internet standard called 'OpenPGP' was created."

"Anyone can write programs conforming to the OpenPGP standard, so anyone else's OpenPGP-compliant programs can be used to exchange encrypted and/or digitally signed data. You don't, strictly speaking, need to decrypt a GnuPG-encrypted with GnuPG, you could use a commercial program--like PGP Software from Zimmermann's old company, or an open source one if you want. However, many people now use the open source project Gnu Privacy Guard, a.k.a. GnuPG."

Bob sips his own drink and settles luxuriously in his seat as he listens, and asks, "Why doesn't everyone use PGP then? Wouldn't it be better to buy software from a company instead of this open source stuff? Couldn't someone hack GnuPG by sticking in some kind of back door? Also, why should I use the command line--isn't there a Windows program I can use? And what about public key encryption?"

"Bob, those are some great questions, but I've had a long day. We're not going to get to Sylvania for another 12 hours, so if you'll excuse me, I'm going to take a nap, and you can look over my notes about using GnuPG and how to use the command line. When I wake up we can talk about public keys. OK?" Sam says as he hands Bob a folder.

"Sure, Sam, I can do that. Thanks!" Bob opens the file and starts to flip through several dozen pages of laser-printed manuscript. "What a nice coincidence that I bump into someone with so much encryption knowledge, just when I need it!" he says, to himself as Sam has already shut his eyes and reclined his seat for a nap.

1.6 COMMAND SUMMARY AND REVIEW

Command	Description and Notes
`gpg --symmetric [filename]` `gpg -c [filename]`	Encrypt using symmetric (secret key) encryption. Filename is optional.
`gpg filename`	If filename is an OpenPGP-compliant file, GnuPG will attempt to verify or decrypt it.
`gpg --decrypt [filename]` `gpg -d [filename]`	Decrypt *filename* (or ASCII-armored text entered interactively). Returns the plaintext to the terminal display.
`gpg --encrypt [filename]` `gpg -e [filename]`	Public key encrypt *filename* (or ASCII-armored text entered interactively).
`gpg --armor --symmetric [filename]` `gpg -ac [filename]`	Encrypt *filename* (or ASCII-armored text entered interactively) using symmetric encryption, and produce ciphertext output to *filename.asc* (or displayed when used interactively).

1.7 REVIEW QUESTIONS

1. Why does Sam know so much about encryption?
2. Should Bob trust Sam?
3. Is there anything about Sam that might be suspicious?

CHAPTER 2

Selected FAQs on Using GnuPG

Bob reads from Sam Mallory's FAQ on using GnuPG:

2.1 WHY USE GnuPG

GnuPG is Free software with a capital "F", which means not only is the program free to download and share, but the source code is also free to download, use and modify. Free software licenses basically say "Do whatever you like with this program--use it, share it, modify it, add to it and fix it, even publish your modifications--as long as you don't change the license agreement." In other words, feel free to add new features to GnuPG and publish them, but you've got to use the same license and allow others to add new features to *your* version of GnuPG and publish them too.

The original PGP was freeware: that meant it was free to download the program but the source code was not published. By 1996 Philip Zimmermann founded PGP Inc. to sell a commercial version of PGP; by 2010 a PGP product line was being marketed by Symantec, and other vendors offer encryption software as well. If you get what you pay for, why do so many people prefer to use a Free program?

The answer is that for encryption, free/open--meaning the source code is freely available and can be reviewed, modified and used without restriction--is best. I feel confident that GnuPG is secure not just because *I* can review the code, but because I know that over the years since its first release, many knowledgeable and skillful programmers and security experts have reviewed the code--and fixed the bugs and errors they've found.

I use software that conforms to the OpenPGP standard because that way I'll always have access to my data. With proprietary data formats, I'm handcuffed to the vendor who controls those formats; I can only access my data as long as I pay the vendor for current software.

Finally, with closed source programs there is concern about vendors including *back doors* that give law enforcement agencies easy access to encrypted data. Though the intention (to defeat criminals) is admirable, the reality is back doors let in anyone who knows about them: not just legitimate law enforcement agents, but also any random hackers, corrupt sheriffs or disgruntled employees who find out about and use the back door, all of which would be bad. Free and open source software is better because no one can secretly add anything to the code base.

Plus, free/open source software doesn't cost anything!

2.2 WHY START WITH THE COMMAND LINE

I'm not saying graphical user interface (GUI) encryption software is bad, I'm just saying that it's best to start out doing encryption at the command line for a number of reasons:

It's the simplest way to get started. Just one thing to download and install (or nothing to install for Linux systems, where GnuPG is already installed).
It works the same, everywhere. If you can use GnuPG at the command line on a Mac, it works almost exactly the same on Linux or Windows.
It mostly works the same as it used to (and as it will in 5 years). No guarantees here, but the GnuPG interface is pretty stable. No need to relearn a new interface when the latest version is released or when it's ported to run under the newest version of Windows or OS X.
GnuPG at the command line is a standard. Much easier to work with a program that is widely available and familiar to anyone who knows about encryption.

Once you understand the basics, it would be counter-productive to stick with the command line, especially if you use encryption regularly. For example, an e-mail reader plug-in to sign and authenticate digital signatures on messages, or a plug-in for a word processor if you frequently encrypt messages you compose.

2.3 WHY USE THE COMMAND LINE

GUIs are the default for modern end-user operating systems, but I prefer using a command line interface (CLI).

The command line is exact; there is no uncertainty about which icon was clicked on (or how many times you clicked), and there's an audit trail that can be used to see what commands were issued[1]. The results of each command can also be viewed easily by scrolling through terminal session window.

There are many programs that act as GUI front-ends to GnuPG, but trying to learn encryption by using them can be as confusing as using the command line version of GnuPG. Also, a GUI front-end adds another point of failure: one more piece of software that can have security flaws or be subverted by an attacker.

Using GnuPG at the command line means stepping through each cryptographic process, which means you can be more aware of what is going on and thus can avoid security pitfalls more easily.

If you find it impossible to use the command line, using an "official" GUI (that is, a GUI program packaged with GnuPG) is acceptable. However, in line with the precept "keep it as simple as possible, but no simpler," using the command line may be preferable where circumstances call for the greatest caution.

2.4 GETTING TO THE COMMAND LINE

On OS X and Linux systems, use the Terminal application to open a CLI. This is the default terminal program for *nix systems; there are other programs that give access to a system shell, which are also acceptable.

The Command Prompt window lets Microsoft Windows users enter commands directly to the system. Command Prompt works similarly to Terminal on OS X/*nix systems.

---

[1]You can scroll old commands with the up and down arrow keys, and view all previous commands via the "history" command (on Windows, `doskey/history`). This can be a risk since anyone looking at your commands can see which files you've been encrypting and decrypting, if you don't clear your history manually. See Chapter 8 for more information.

Getting to the command line:

Windows: from the Start icon, choose "All Programs," then "Accessories," then "Command Prompt."
OS X: the Terminal application is found in the Applications/ Utilities folder.
Linux: the Terminal application can be started by pressing the Ctrl-Alt-T key combination, or from the Applications menu.

Many shell commands that make life easier on those systems are unavailable in Windows. I recommend using an OS X/*nix system for cryptography; Windows users can use a live-boot version of Linux to get the same functionality, with improved overall security.

2.5 IS GnuPG EVEN INSTALLED?

Checking whether GnuPG is installed is a good introduction to using GnuPG: it calls for entering a GnuPG command and checking the result. To see whether GnuPG is installed, open a terminal or command line window and issue the command (type the command and press <Enter>):

```
$ gpg --version
```

The command prompt is the dollar sign ($). The prompt is what tells you the computer is ready to accept a command; the exact prompt you see will almost certainly look different. On Windows, it looks like c:\Users\Sam>; on OS X, Linux, and other UNIX-like systems the default prompt usually includes *hostname* (name of the computer you're using), the *path* (current working directory, as with Windows), and your user ID on the system, ending with the $ symbol. Like this:

```
sams-laptop:myDocs sam$
```

This prompt tells me that I'm logged into a *nix/OS X system as "sam," on "sams-laptop," in the "myDocs" directory.

To execute a command, type the command and press the Enter key.

The output from the command gpg --version will look something like this:

```
gpg (GnuPG) 2.0.19 (Gpg4win 2.1.1-34299-beta)
libgcrypt 1.5.0
Copyright (C) 2012 Free Software Foundation, Inc.
License GPLv3+: GNU GPL version 3 or later <http://gnu.org/licenses/gpl.html>
This is free software: you are free to change and redistribute it.
There is NO WARRANTY, to the extent permitted by law.

Home: C:/Users/Sam/AppData/Roaming/gnupg
Supported algorithms:
Pubkey: RSA, ELG, DSA
Cipher: 3DES, CAST5, BLOWFISH, AES, AES192, AES256, TWOFISH, CAMELLIA128,
        CAMELLIA192, CAMELLIA256
Hash: MD5, SHA1, RIPEMD160, SHA256, SHA384, SHA512, SHA224
Compression: Uncompressed, ZIP, ZLIB, BZIP2
```

GnuPG reports back what version it's running, in this case GnuPG version 2.0.19/GnuPG for Windows (Gpg4win) version 2.1.1-34299-beta. GnuPG reports more than version about itself in response to this command: where the GnuPG home directory[2] is and which cryptographic algorithms are supported: listed after Pubkey are the public key algorithms being used, listed next under Cipher are the single key algorithms, under Hash for secure hashing and under Compression for compression algorithms[3].

GnuPG comes in two flavors: version 1 (currently at release 1.4.12) is the "portable standalone version," and version 2 (currently at 2.0.19) is "enhanced." Both versions give essentially the same user experience and both are current and supported, so whichever version is installed should be acceptable.

To see which is the most current version of GnuPG, check the GnuPG web site, http://www.gnupg.org/.

2.6 GnuPG COMMANDS AND OPTIONS

One enters GnuPG commands at the system command line (Linux or Mac OS X terminal or Windows command prompt). They can be

---

[2]The directory C:\Users\Sam\AppData\Roaming\gnupg is the GnuPG home directory on a Windows system; it would be ~/.gnupg (a hidden directory in the user's home directory) under OS X or Linux.

[3]By default, GnuPG compresses files before encrypting; according to the specification in RFC 4880, "compression has the added side effect that some types of attacks can be thwarted by the fact that slightly altered, compressed data rarely uncompresses without severe errors."

tricky to get right, but using the command line makes it easier to understand what GnuPG is doing, and makes it easier to do the "right" thing (where "right" = "what I want it to do").

Checking for the software version is a simple method I can use to check whether GnuPG is installed; the next command I want to know is how to get help:

```
$ gpg --help
```

The `gpg --help` (or `gpg -h`) command summarizes commonly used GnuPG commands and options, and returns the same information as `gpg --version`, followed by a summary of GnuPG commands and options, starting with basic syntax rules for using it at the command line:

```
Syntax: gpg [options] [files]
sign, check, encrypt or decrypt
default operation depends on the input data
```

In other words, to invoke GnuPG, enter one or more options (or none), give it one or more files (or none) as needed; if an action (command) is not specified, GnuPG will choose a default action depending on the options and files that are specified.

NOTE: *Using explicit commands and options will produce the best results with GnuPG, as it allows me to specify exactly what I want GnuPG to do. However, explicit commands are not always necessary.*

GnuPG commands issued with a filename but without a specific command are interpreted in context of the file contents. If the file contains GnuPG data (e.g., if the file is encrypted or digitally signed), then GnuPG will do the "right thing" with the file: decrypt the file or verify the signature.

The rest of the help file contains a list of GnuPG commands (actions that the program can perform for me). This is the actual list that `gpg --help` displays; don't worry if they seem confusing,

I only really use a half dozen or so commands on a regular basis, and a few more less frequently:

```
-s, --sign make a signature
    --clearsign make a clear text signature
-b, --detach-sign make a detached signature
-e, --encrypt encrypt data
-c, --symmetric encryption only with symmetric cipher
-d, --decrypt decrypt data (default)
    --verify verify a signature
-k, --list-keys list keys
    --list-sigs list keys and signatures
    --check-sigs list and check key signatures
    --fingerprint list keys and fingerprints
-K, --list-secret-keys list secret keys
    --gen-key generate a new key pair
    --gen-revoke generate a revocation certificate
    --delete-keys remove keys from the public keyring
    --delete-secret-keys remove keys from the secret keyring
    --sign-key sign a key
    --lsign-key sign a key locally
    --edit-key sign or edit a key
    --passwd change a passphrase
    --export export keys
    --send-keys export keys to a key server
    --recv-keys import keys from a key server
    --search-keys search for keys on a key server
    --refresh-keys update all keys from a keyserver
    --import import/merge keys
    --card-status print the card status
    --card-edit change data on a card
    --change-pin change a card's PIN
    --update-trustdb update the trust database
    --print-md print message digests
    --server run in server mode
```

Every command has a long-form name like: --encrypt, --verify, or --list-keys. These long command names are prefixed with the double-dash and are relatively easy to understand. Some commands also have a short-form name; for example, -e for "encrypt," -s for "sign," or -k for "list keys."

I can have GnuPG sign and encrypt at the same time, but all other GnuPG actions are strictly one action at a time (e.g., list keys, decrypt data, export a key, etc.).

After listing the commands themselves, help lists all GnuPG options. As with commands, most users can get away with knowing only three or four of these:

```
Options:

-a, --armor create ascii armored output
-r, --recipient USER-ID encrypt for USER-ID
-u, --local-user USER-ID use USER-ID to sign or decrypt
-z N set compress level to N (0 disables)
    --textmode use canonical text mode
-o, --output FILE write output to FILE
-v, --verbose verbose
-n, --dry-run do not make any changes
-i, --interactive prompt before overwriting
    --openpgp use strict OpenPGP behavior
```

Followed by a handful of examples:

```
-se -r Bob [file] sign and encrypt for user Bob
--clearsign [file] make a clear text signature
--detach-sign [file] make a detached signature
--list-keys [names] show keys
--fingerprint [names] show fingerprints
```

It's easier to understand if you look at examples.

2.7 SIMPLE EXAMPLES

To encrypt (single key) a file:

```
$ gpg -c essay.txt
$
```

Other than the prompts to enter a passphrase, GnuPG returns no additional information, and writes the ciphertext to a file called essay.txt.gpg. The original plaintext file (essay.txt) remains on disk.

To decrypt a symmetric key-encrypted file and save the plaintext to a file:

```
$ gpg --output example.docx --decrypt example.docx.gpg
gpg: CAST5 encrypted data
gpg: encrypted with 1 passphrase
gpg: WARNING: message was not integrity protected
```

The command entered above can be read as "decrypt file example.docx.gpg and write the plaintext into file example.docx." When executed, the plaintext file example.docx is created after the user successfully enters the passphrase. The WARNING message indicates that although the file was encrypted, it was not digitally signed.

2.8 OPTIONS: GETTING MORE INFORMATION

GnuPG messages can be terse, and even though the program reads or writes a file, it may not "report back" with any messages (e.g., what actually happened). To get GnuPG to return more information about results, use the verbose option (-v):

```
$ gpg -v -c foo.bar
gpg: using cipher CAST5
gpg: writing to `foo.bar.gpg'
$
```

This tells me GnuPG encrypted the file with the CAST5 algorithm (the default for symmetric encryption) and wrote an encrypted file as foo.bar.gpg.

Verbose mode does not affect the function of the program, just the amount of information returned by GnuPG when it executes a command.

"Doubling" the verbose mode option increases the amount of information returned. If I specify the -vv option for this command, I get no more information—there isn't any. Increasing amounts of information is often available for other GnuPG commands, and can be accessed by using more v's at the command line (e.g., gpg -vvvv -c foo.bar).

2.9 OPTIONS: TEXT OR BINARY

When GnuPG creates cryptographic output (e.g., when it encrypts a file, exports a public key, generates a digital signature), the default behavior is to save the output to a binary file with the extension .gpg. As noted above, it is also possible to output to a differently named file relatively easily, but it will still be saved as a binary file.

Binary files are fine, but it's often better to produce human-readable output. For example, when a digital signature is appended to an e-mail or other text message, the signature must consist only of characters that can be displayed correctly by the e-mail or other application software. This is why there is an option in GnuPG to generate output that encodes all the cryptographic data in a form that can be displayed in readable form.

The --armor (-a) option directs GnuPG to "create ASCII-armored output." Armored output simplifies matters when sending encrypted data in an e-mail message, or when publishing public keys[4].

To encrypt symmetrically to an ASCII-armored file, I use this command:

```
$ gpg --armor -c foo.bar
```

The default output file is foo.bar.asc (.asc indicates that the file contains ASCII data). That file can be viewed with any text editor—or listed at the command line with shell commands like cat, less or more:

```
$ cat foo.bar.asc
-----BEGIN PGP MESSAGE-----

jA0EAwMC+Y3fEGr12USryUf0TXaBC1zPg63rBu6jUm4iwkYC1B9xFyKsCSLHY7O1
GXuIUeCHwMLOs+LbVE7/tC1MsDgnE2ZC3ZA1A2thh8xS0y/3jGNN3g==
=ncY8
-----END PGP MESSAGE-----
```

ASCII-armored results can be saved to a file, cut and pasted into a message, or printed out and manually re-entered to a computer for decryption later. You could even take a photo of the output; this kind of screenshot might be enough to fly under the radar of an attacker looking for suspicious files.

ASCII armor is particularly useful when experimenting with GnuPG.

---

[4]For more about ASCII armoring, see http://tools.ietf.org/html/rfc4880#section-6.2.

2.10 COMMAND SUMMARY AND REVIEW

Command	Description and Notes
gpg --version	Get version information about GnuPG.
gpg --help gpg -h	Get brief summary of commonly used GnuPG commands.
gpg --output *filename1* --decrypt *[filename2]* gpg -o filename -d *[filename]*	Decrypt *filename2* (or ciphertext entered interactively) and write the plaintext to *filename1*.
gpg -v --symmetric *[filename]* gpg -vc *[filename]*	Encrypt *filename* (or plaintext entered interactively) with first-level verbose messages.
gpg --armor --symmetric *[filename]* gpg -ac *[filename]*	Encrypt *filename* (or plaintext entered interactively) using ASCII armor. If a file, write ciphertext to *filename.asc* (if interactively, ciphertext will be displayed in the terminal window).

2.11 REVIEW QUESTIONS

1. Practice some of the command line commands introduced in this chapter, including one to get a listing of all files in a directory, and to list a file's contents on screen. Look up how to copy a file at the command line of your OS, how to delete a file, and how to use wildcards to do things to multiple files with a single command.
2. What is a FAQ? What is a Howto document? Why do you think Sam is compiling a FAQ on how to use GnuPG?

CHAPTER 3

Public Keys

Bob's eyes fluttered shut reading Sam's howto, but he twitches into awareness when Sam's wristwatch emits a tiny beep, just 20 minutes into their flight.

"OK sleepyhead, are you ready for more GnuPG?" Sam asks.

Bob, brushing sleep from his eyes, answers, "Sure. Can you explain how to do public key encryption now?"

Sam answers: "Public key encryption is the real thing. Strong cryptography scared the US government back in the 1990s because it's so strong. With my public key, you can encrypt a message to me and as long as I can keep my private key safe, I am the only person in the world who can decrypt that message."

Bob asks, "But why is that so scary?"

Sam, leaning forward, says, "That first thing I showed you, how to encrypt a file with a secret key, is good enough for some purposes, but what happens when you need to send off a secret file to someone--let's call her 'Alice'--on the other side of the world? There's no safe way for you to share a secret key with her."

"That's funny, my American friend's name is Alice," says Bob. Sam goes on:

"You can talk to Alice on the phone, send e-mail or texts, go on chat forums--but they're all insecure, especially in a place like Sylvania where the government always listens." Bob involuntarily peers over his shoulder; Sam goes on. "You can't give her a passphrase by phone or e-mail or text, because an eavesdropper can snoop it. But if you have Alice's public key (or if you can get it) you can encrypt a message to her without anyone being able to read it, and without risking an eavesdropper intercepting a decryption key."

"*That's* why public key crypto is so scary to governments: if you have Alice's public key, and if Alice keeps her key safe, you can encrypt messages to her confidentially that only Alice will be able to decrypt," Sam continues. "Even *you* can't decrypt the messages you send her!"

Sam goes on, "On the Internet, you've got to worry about what an eavesdropper--let's call her, um, 'Eve'—does. That's just a cryptographic convention, like 'Bob' and 'Alice' for two people who want to communicate securely." Sam pauses imperceptibly as Bob mutters to himself: "Eve, that's my wife's name. ..."

Ignoring Bob's apparent discomfort, Sam continues, "You don't want Eve to see any of your messages, but with public key encryption, even if she knows the public key you're using, Eve *still* can't read the plaintext--unless she can get Alice's private key."

"But can she, Eve I mean, figure out who I'm sending messages to?" Bob asks.

Sam thinks for a moment. "It all depends on how closely Eve is tracking you. If she's logging your Internet traffic, she'll know you're sending ciphertext and she can tell to whom you're sending e-mail. That's actually the best-case scenario, too: Eve could have a keylogger running[1] in which case she can get your passphrases and everything else you type at that computer."

Bob asks, "Then using encryption would be pointless. Is there nothing I can do?"

"It's not exactly pointless," Sam crosses his legs as he answers. "Encryption is only part of being secure. You can communicate

---

[1]*Keystroke logging* is the practice of capturing all keystrokes entered at a computer and saving them for retrieval and analysis. A *keylogger* can be a piece of software installed on the system, or it could be a hardware device installed surreptitiously. If you think you're being keylogged, you could have some serious problems (either someone actually is too interested in your computing activities, or you are delusional).

securely with Alice, and keep your secrets from Eve, as long as you take other precautions. But you still want to encrypt your messages, so if your other measures fail your data is still private."

"What kind of measures?" asks Bob.

"Well, you can avoid network scanners by using a public network, like at a public library, coffee shop, or Internet cafe[2]. To protect against keylogging, there are various anti-keylogger programs floating around. I wouldn't worry too much; even in Sylvania you don't get 'special attention' unless you're doing something to attract attention. But your data can still be sniffed on the network, so keeping a low profile is always a good idea." Sam opens his laptop again, and says, "Let's take a look at how to encrypt to someone's public key. Why don't you open a terminal window on your laptop, Bob."

Bob pulls his battered Sylvanian laptop out from under his seat, and says, "But Sam, I don't have any public key myself. How would that work?"

"Actually, you don't need your own public key to do public key encryption, just the public key of the person you're sending the message or file to. So let's start out with you getting *my* public key, and you can encrypt a file and send it to me," Sam says, "I've setup a tethered mobile wi-fi hotspot, let me show you. . ." as he helps Bob connect.

3.1 GETTING SOMEONE'S PUBLIC KEY

Sam sends Bob a link (http://crypto.loshin.com/my.public.key.asc/) and says, "You've got GnuPG installed and ready to go; just go to my link and you'll see my public key[3]. What I want you to do is copy that whole public key block, starting from the first hyphen of the first line, and ending just after the last hyphen of the last line. In your browser window, highlight the whole thing (on Windows, press <Ctrl-c>, on a Mac press <Command-c>, on Linux, just leave the key highlighted

---

[2]To be really safe, consider MAC spoofing. See Reverse Engineering Forensics (http://crypto. loshin.com/2013/01/17/reverse-engineering-forensics/) for more information.
[3]Or, download it from a public keyserver, and compare it to the key at the URL provided; that makes it harder for an attacker to fake a public key. For more about keyservers, see Chapter 6.

when you switch to the terminal window). The public key I'm pointing you to looks like this":

```
-----BEGIN PGP PUBLIC KEY BLOCK-----

mQENBFD1u2UBCADNwvLGUnivhWrL+UtpkohaZXpdwCbO8cKVf3aeLsTZi8iP2bKT
/LaopR+tr+mA4AwU5biHBrm7FHLrBef49qUqiCI7v0vjlH7NBEEfIZwscnMZUjke
EVNE7g+Ag+yJLCNaMJRuTuSLoDV4gIevIZgJ1TFwpHoXoo17304xIgr4R75qkIPg
5I5GMRXZ+MSlerEAanfrTG8HFeNhPaOrLKj4GzJr+SAdOqVuLp+DNfixCAhGHmpR
HcQLCgFqpAanFSOGgFRxRMoo2Gu7Kw5rqHu5N3v4H2h+Q2jaHSYDw9UHzBkD4ZRJ
IdC+AXgpZ1K/+ghy9jXsNohilefJ7akMLM7jABEBAAG0P1NhbSBNYWxsb3J5IChQ
ZXJzb25hbCBDdGc1ldG9ncmFwaHkpIDxzYW0ubWFsbG9yeS40MDRAZ21haWwuY29t
PokBPwQTAQIAKQUCUPW7ZQIbAwUJBKKGAAcLCQgHAwIBBhUIAgkKCwQWAgMBAh4B
AheAAAoJEDs7s7MaD3Ea3hIH/i2Gpt951eboWUp480dWJr5ZfaKpkgWA+aDWN2K6
D1fo3NkxrOiD5U2fdfrAaCBeA4iAL9flBQiYjmep6dY6oupmHODvS+euYl5rsTOl
Ey7WRhGqJ+HjQ6tc2/wfgVi/QS2vLtHn9Hr6LDg8QoIyfVTfDd6x+k1Bk3n02yOh
Ruz70vUTiW8XSiFWlKoK2JFa3gjdRJW7CoK4ZF1HLX8O9mJEvQOwVB0BVP1XMfQn
1+2Y+w2CdgHJ/HklLxp7u39F8eixS9cfx1jILibMATxhkV9Y3BjrCZY4NM1JQL/F
GTo59BzTkoGIyKfgML13WWhgca3qoFE77IJ3dzKKRgaEVb65AQ0EUPW7ZQEIAJXF
+iJ2U5+56rwq64x3GsT8SebhRXYfapdllHTryYxKaPs6FROTthpFevSKrCOEwnSi
1sW2EEUCKZ+oSUYcOqxMs0ugTYu2WXtSZNA6n1LARZIRrNmvjicOYm5GJDsUmz1y
nUkmde9qLsgc9f5oEvsRbGh3CIVko8gDapnnO2NWA76zUhgEXC7tA5fzkEtWYN3E
CSJjKMqwiSxHhjsNfQE4tyranXnsOAx0RuseD/zyNUuKe+Cl+NDDHR15YtSwDMUw
ZU7eWDIp0vkRkfzKX0nFVYVwDvrP36uUhtjU2aPhfvf6bxhrnzxYSswsyf0HyQdVw
2GblWF/nSvNAXYrUEpEAEQEAAYkBJQQYAQIADwUCUPW7ZQIbDAUJBKKGAAAKCRA7
O7OzGg9xGs3VB/0QP8xfjDCOthQd57EAuntkJ+hN5cI8mRZGo540+vleI8qO1WYe
HjTMeTe1karIdDHbDOPFYAdA1F6OcD/jbCSObBHr2RsNfHSMeN5MLFZY9Uwepf1y
DEgC5Cjei5TY2oQJKIKrmF2egtP3e+RgDszNoDaFM6+m+I2703qGTeSXa1VUUd9Q
1EXCHbWZYedu+pmBkRQaEqPo0ug4kMfuctew35n56eF32hzlU1paEoqGsggdW8Q/
I7bUUOZ8hJqPfMLNe5IZge2j211A/ZQQH39RxVJCnaqgrkxCWI99PvvkF89W29mD
AgW6nCFtEZnn/4bMEWfwf452TCQmvWR/ajN9
=qxpG
-----END PGP PUBLIC KEY BLOCK-----
```

"Now, in the terminal window, enter the GnuPG command `gpg --import`; when you hit <Enter>, you'll get the same sort of nothing as we did before when we were encrypting interactively. Then paste the public key[4]. You'll see that big chunk of text, with the flashing cursor at the end of the last line. Then, press <Enter> once, then the 'end-of-file' character[5]." Bob followed along, and was rewarded with this output from GnuPG:

```
gpg: key 1A0F711A: public key "Sam Mallory <sam.mallory.404@gmail.com>" imported
gpg: Total number processed: 1
gpg:               imported: 1  (RSA: 1)
```

Sam says, "That's what it looks like when the public key is imported the first time; if you already had my key in your keyring, GnuPG would try to update the key and return a message about it being updated (if

---

[4] <Ctrl-v> on Windows, <Command-v> on a Macintosh or middle mouse click on Linux.
[5] Ctrl-z on Windows, Ctrl-d on OS X/Linux.

something in my key had changed) or a message that the key is unchanged. If the public key wasn't valid, you'd get a message, and so on."

"Now," Sam says, "you've got my public key in your keyring so you can do public key encryption, but only with me, for now. Type your essay in at the command line to encrypt it. Start by entering the command `gpg -ao essay.gpg -r 'Sam Mallory' -e` and press <Enter>, then type in the essay, and after the last line press <Enter> and 'end-of-file'."

Bob says "This seems so complicated," as he types in the terminal window:

```
$ gpg -ao essay.gpg -r 'Sam Mallory' -e
Free Sylvania!
Now is the time for all good men to come to the aid of their country!
```

"Nothing seems to have happened," Bob says.

"Actually, a lot happened," says Sam, "but let's translate the command. It starts with `gpg`--start GnuPG; then, two options, `-a` (for ASCII-armored output) and `-o` (short for `--output`) tells GnuPG to write ciphertext to the filename that follows, `essay.gpg`."

Sam continues. "Then we get to `-r`, short for `--recipient`, which means I want to specify a recipient from my keyring. It can be a name, an e-mail address, or key ID. In this case, you typed in the name, in quotes, from the public key you just imported[6]. Finally, you specified the `-e` command (short for `--encrypt`) telling GnuPG to encrypt to the recipient's public key. Then GnuPG encrypts and writes the result to the file."

"One way to 'read' this command is to start from the last part: 'Do public key encryption using the public key for Sam Mallory, and output the result with ASCII-armor, into a file called `essay.gpg`'."

Sam sips from his champagne flute and says, "GnuPG took the data you entered, encrypted it with my public key, and wrote ASCII-armored ciphertext into the file. Do a directory listing for files with the extensions.gpg, and you'll see--the command would be `ls *.gpg` (or `dir *.gpg` on Windows)."

---

[6]Also acceptable would have been `sam.mallory.404@gmail.com` (the e-mail address associated with that key) or `1A0F711A` (key ID).

This is what Bob saw:

```
$ ls *.gpg
essay.gpg
```

Sam says, "I suggested using ASCII armor so it would be easy to see what an encrypted file looks like; also, you could just paste the contents of the file into an e-mail. Use the `cat` command and you can see what's in that file":

```
$ cat essay.gpg
-----BEGIN PGP MESSAGE-----

hQEMAyETvsDdu2pNAQf/TuPHs8tPDi7IW3o+Wzzsg80gwNXjmfe4ec5V9LhcdgU9
MoFr3U/zEl0zEqeH1Z4HtdTzlBkPvswpYlHLFbFqNWtsncsTdX0njnCqbOQbtFrc
gLbl8nOBaYmnMhDQNJxVrpRAbPzs6HpuYHMSe6VSj+B6dSG+TNLdvg9N4k8V+q8p
EJuyvmATq4UnPXjN8Y7CEG19N5zpE+52a4ymoYmAmTSKb71VC1Ed1E4IcA6AUOys
zfAsSciPbEEjxzKtUsPyHFXCjtPiWf5IUAlHMFaNq0Ef7NTgBo56zxvwKgI4dvlI
tJT0allLD2Ax4uVeBjmmRyRS3nYsVepm9KXk8OTNzNJxARHrXjiyM1jqlXlszpp1
eYv9IvOToqXtFU0cBSRNCTwW7TeEwlqyfzreUCRbOLWzB6N01viG6VK6xjDtFHXo
/Y1A4IXgsrwUPA9MaGyDo8m4HiwvZQ3n7Opfxq/JU85OXTF3m4oHuY49ZVsSZw4n
R54=
=YpFz
-----END PGP MESSAGE-----
```

As he looks over the ciphertext, Bob asks, "So, how can I decrypt this?"

"*You* can't decrypt it at all. Only I can decrypt it, with my own private key. And since you did it interactively, there's no file on your computer with the essay on it. And before you ask, as long as you delete (securely) the ciphertext file after you send it to me, no one should be able to link you to that file," Sam answers.

Sam continues, "If you wanted to just generate the ciphertext, without creating a file, you could do that, too. Enter the command without the -o option":

```
$ gpg -ar 'Sam Mallory' -e
```

"and type in the same essay, and you get the ciphertext output to the screen. You can then copy the ciphertext from inside the command line window and paste it into any other window. So, you could paste it into an e-mail message, or drop it into an input field on a web site, or just print it out."

Bob ponders and says, "OK, that makes sense, but I'm still unclear on what a public key pair is. How do I get my own? What can I do with it?"

3.2 GENERATING A PUBLIC KEY

"It's pretty simple to generate a public key pair, but it's also pretty easy to mess things up if you're not careful when you do it," says Sam. "People *think* it's complicated because you're prompted for a lot of information that seems complicated when you do it. And you can make it complicated, if you know what you want. To create your first key pair, enter `gpg --key-gen` at the command line, and start reading the prompts":

```
$ gpg --key-gen

gpg (GnuPG/MacGPG2) 2.0.18; Copyright (C) 2011 Free Software Foundation, Inc.
This is free software: you are free to change and redistribute it.
There is NO WARRANTY, to the extent permitted by law.

Please select what kind of key you want:
   (1) RSA and RSA (default)
   (2) DSA and Elgamal
   (3) DSA (sign only)
   (4) RSA (sign only)
Your selection?
```

Sam points to the prompt and says, "GnuPG prompts you through the process, giving options for each question. The default options are usually good enough for most purposes, especially when you're starting out. You accept the default by hitting <Enter>, making it even easier."

"What does 'RSA and RSA' mean?" asks Bob. "Should I know what that means?"

Sam says, "RSA is the name of a public key encryption algorithm. The name comes from the discoverers of the algorithm—Ron Rivest, Adi Shamir, and Leonard Adleman. Wikipedia (http://en.wikipedia. org/wiki/RSA_(algorithm)) is an OK place to start researching--they explain the basics well enough. The differences between RSA and the other options (DSA, ElGamal) are technical, but the consensus is that RSA is better. It became the default algorithm what it was released into the public domain by the patent holder, RSA Security, in 2000. Prior to that, it was protected by patent, putting it off-limits to free/ open source software developers who've got to avoid using any code or algorithm limited by intellectual property rights."

"But why is it there twice?" asks Bob.

"GnuPG uses one public key pair for encryption, and another for digital signatures," answers Sam. "You'd think one pair would be enough, but it's not."

3.3 WHY TWO KEY PAIRS?

Sam continues: "There are good reasons for using two separate key pairs. First, if you'll allow an oversimplification, the technical reason: signing and encrypting are the same function, but with private and public keys swapped. So if I use just one public/private key pair when I sign something, I'm actually 'encrypting' it with my private key. That signature can be 'decrypted' (actually, authenticated) with my public key."

"If an attacker can get me to sign a plaintext with my private key, and encrypt the same plaintext with my public key, it opens up some vulnerabilities." Sam continues: "If I use the same key for signing and encryption, and if an attacker can get me to sign some of my own encrypted data, then I'm actually decrypting my own ciphertext. That's an oversimplification, but the threat is easily avoided by using separate keys."

"The practical reasons for two pairs make sense, too. For one thing, it makes sense for organizations to keep signing and encryption key pairs separate. If I have people sending me encrypted data on behalf of an organization, the organization will need access to the private key (i.e., in the event of my death or 'termination'). Even if it's just myself, it's good practice to update the public key for encryption from time to time--just as it's good practice to keep the signature key stable over time."

Bob asks, "But why change the encryption key more often?"

Sam answers, "Keeping my signature key stable makes for longer term continuity: you should be able to authenticate something I signed years ago. Changing the encryption key more frequently means that if someone exposes my private encryption key for something I encrypted years ago, that won't automatically give the attacker access to more recent ciphertexts."

"So," says Sam, "pick the default, RSA/RSA, and let's move on."

3.4 KEY LENGTH

"The next question is how long a key to use," says Sam, as Bob presses <Enter> and gets the next prompt:

```
RSA keys may be between 1024 and 4096 bits long.
What keysize do you want? (2048)
Requested keysize is 2048 bits
```

"Should I pick the longest possible key length for more security?" Bob asks.

Sam explains: "Key length, like many options, represents a tradeoff. 'More security' usually means 'less convenience' or 'less easy to use'. Key length is no different: a 4096-bit key means a cumbersome public key (it's longer!) and longer processing times. Of course, the shortest key you can choose is easier and faster, but shorter keys are also more vulnerable to brute-force attacks, particularly over the years as the available processing power to run a brute-force attack grows."

"For most users, especially beginners, 2048 bits should be plenty."

Bob hits <Enter> again to accept the default value, and more dialog appears:

```
Requested keysize is 2048 bits
Please specify how long the key should be valid.
         0 = key does not expire
      <n>  = key expires in n days
      <n>w = key expires in n weeks
      <n>m = key expires in n months
      <n>y = key expires in n years
Key is valid for? (0)
```

Sam says, "Now comes an important choice: when will your key expire."

3.5 KEY EXPIRATION AND KEY REVOCATION

"Why would I want my key to expire?" asks Bob. "It seems as though it would be a hassle to always be updating keys."

"Great question. The short answer is, you likely *do* want at least some keys to expire, and any key pair that doesn't expire on its own, you should always be able to revoke your key as soon as possible if you find out it's been compromised," answers Sam. "This is where the default value--never expire[7]--is not your best choice for how long your key should be valid, ESPECIALLY if you're starting out with GnuPG--because when you're starting out, you're going to mess things up."

Bob asks, "Messing up, how?"

"For one thing, it's pretty easy to forget a passphrase, especially if you've picked a strong one but haven't written it down and stored it somewhere safe. Or, even if you picked a passphrase that you thought you could remember, it's easy to forget if you don't use it often enough." says Sam. He continues:

"For this part of the key generation process, you either hit <Enter> for no expiration, OR you enter a number by itself as the number of days until the key expires, OR a number plus the letter w (for weeks), m (for months), or y (for years). So, for a two-week key pair you'd enter 2w here; for a 10-year key pair, enter 10y, and so on."

"It's a good idea when you're starting out to use keys with short lifetimes. That way you don't have to worry about forgetting your passphrase and going through life with a public key pair that you can't use or control. Also, it makes fiddling around with them less stressful if you know the key pair dies in a day or two."

Bob, still uncertain, says, "So, to try a one-day key I just enter 1, right?"

"Exactly," says Sam. "Try it, and don't forget to answer is this correct?":

```
Please specify how long the key should be valid.
         0 = key does not expire
      <n>  = key expires in n days
      <n>w = key expires in n weeks
      <n>m = key expires in n months
      <n>y = key expires in n years
Key is valid for? (0) 1
Key expires at Mon Nov 12 10:49:56 2013 EST
Is this correct? (y/N) y
```

"Very important to note here, Bob, even if you do set an expiration for the key, you should also create a *revocation certificate* for any key

---

[7]GnuPG developers may be fixing this sequence of prompts (as of 2013), so pay attention when you generate a new key!

you use for sensitive data. The revocation certificate lets you notify users the key is no good anymore."

Bob asks, "What does *revocation* actually mean?"

Sam says, "Revoking a key is basically announcing to the world that you're not using the key anymore, and telling people 'don't use this key to encrypt anything for me'. This assumes the people encrypting messages to you check the keyservers regularly, but people *should* check for updates on their keyrings every now and then. And if not, when you revoke a key, notify anyone who's used the old one."

"And why would I want to revoke a key?" asks Bob.

3.6 REASONS FOR KEY REVOCATION

Sam, clearly savoring the conversation, says, "People revoke keys for different reasons, sometimes by plan and sometimes not. Some people change encryption keys periodically to improve security or use different keys for different reasons. More keys mean more problems for an attacker to solve, making it harder to break any particular ciphertext. Some people change keys over longer periods: key length ranges for strong encryption get longer as computers get more powerful. In 1991, 512-bit keys were considered (marginally) acceptable, twenty-some years later, 2048-bit keys are considered acceptable for most purposes, with 1024 bits being the minimum and 4096 bits being the maximum."

"People revoke keys when they change organizational affiliation or when they change e-mail address. I call these revocations *planned* because the transition is expected and the revoker can announce the key change in advance." Sam pauses and says, "These cases allow changes to happen in an orderly way, with advance warning of the change and time to distribute new keys and revoke old keys."

"Unplanned revocations are different: you have to revoke a key if you somehow lost control over it, like by forgetting your passphrase or having a computer with the key on it stolen. In those cases, it's more important to act promptly because if you lose control over your key, your attacker might be able to read your secret mail (if an encryption key is compromised) or sign your messages (if a signing key is compromised)--or both, if someone cracks your key pair passphrase. In this case, the sooner you notify the world of the revocation, the better."

Sam continues: "But you know how I said you should revoke your key if you forget your passphrase? You can't generate a revocation certificate without your passphrase! So the best practice is to generate a revocation certificate right after you generate the key, and then store the certificate somewhere safe. That way, even if you lose the passphrase, you can still revoke the key."

"If you're going to use GnuPG for protection, you do need to be careful about managing your public key, as well as keeping it safe." Sam says, "Later, I'll show you how to do key revocation[8]. But now, let's finish generating *this* key!"

3.7 GENERATING A PUBLIC KEY PAIR, COMPLETED

Bob types in a y and <Enter> to approve the key being good for just one day, and:

```
GnuPG needs to construct a user ID to identify your key.

Real name: Bob Wobble
Email address: bobwobble2@gmail.com
Comment:
```

"Your last name is 'Wobble'? That's an unusual name," says Sam.

"Actually, 'Wobble' is a very common name in Sylvania. What kind of comment should I put in here?" asks Bob.

"The comment is optional, but it can be very helpful when you actively use more than one public key. You could specify different keys for use on different computers, in which case you could put the computer name in the comment. Or, you might use different keys for different purposes, for example, one key for work encryption and another for friends," says Sam, and with a leer, "or for 'special friends', like, say, your special American friend, Alice, eh?"

---

[8]See Chapter 7.

Bob offers Sam no more reaction than a blank stare as he says, "I think I'll just put 'test #1' in there; it will expire in a day anyway."

```
Comment: test #1
You selected this USER-ID:
    "Bob Wobble (test #1) <bobwobble2@gmail.com>"

Change (N)ame, (C)omment, (E)mail or (O)kay/(Q)uit? o
You need a Passphrase to protect your secret key.
```

Sam points to Bob's screen and says, "See how the GUI pops up a little dialog box to enter your passphrase? Like when we encrypted before: enter the passphrase, then enter it again, and then GnuPG asks for some randomness from you."

```
We need to generate a lot of random bytes. It is a good idea to perform
some other action (type on the keyboard, move the mouse, utilize the
disks) during the prime generation; this gives the random number
generator a better chance to gain enough entropy.
```

"At this point, you could type randomly in a word processor, or just wiggle your mouse around on the screen for a while," says Sam, as he waits a moment for Bob to follow the instructions. "You're just about done, now."

```
gpg: key 51266592 marked as ultimately trusted
public and secret key created and signed.

gpg: checking the trustdb
gpg: 3 marginal(s) needed, 1 complete(s) needed, PGP trust model
gpg: depth: 0  valid:   6  signed:   0  trust: 0 -, 0q, 0n, 0m, 0f, 6u
gpg: next trustdb check due at 2013-01-20
pub   2048R/51266592 2013-01-19 [expires: 2013-01-20]
      Key fingerprint = 3835 6BF3 AA97 48C9 173B  DEA5 6198 1C18 5126 6592
uid                    Bob Wobble (test #1) <bobwobble2@gmail.com>
sub   2048R/87F6DF54 2013-01-19 [expires: 2013-01-20]

$
```

"And you're done!" Sam points to the screen again. "See where it says pub there after the lines that start gpg? That's where GnuPG gives you information about your *primary key* of your new key pair":

2048R identifies the key as a 2048-bit RSA key

51266592 the key ID, to identify the key when you're encrypting or signing

2013-01-19 is the date the key was created

[expires: 2013-01-20] is when the key expires

"The next line is the *key fingerprint*, which is a more complete identifier (notice that the last eight characters of the fingerprint are the same as the key ID), then the next line lists the name, comment, and e-mail address you entered, followed by a line starting with sub, for the *subkey*." Sam looks at Bob and continues, "Most people use the primary key (the first one listed) to do their signing, and one or more subkeys for encrypting."

Sam pauses as he thinks about what he's just said. "You've got to remember, though, that you don't use your *own* subkey for encrypting data for others--the subkey is what other people use to encrypt data that they are sending to *you*. So you might give your wife one subkey and a different one for your 'special friend'; that way, you know anything encrypted with your wife's subkey is either coming from your wife, or from someone who got the public key from your wife. I can show you how to do that later, if you like."

Bob thinks it over, clearly waging an internal battle over whether to be offended or interested; he then changes the subject: "That comment I used, I don't like it. Should I even bother with the comment?"

"People use comments because you can have more than one key with the same name/e-mail address. If you assign unique comments to each key, you can pick the one you want by the comment value instead of the key ID," explains Sam.

"So, Bob, now you've got a public key pair to play with, at least until it expires tomorrow. The next step is to 'publish' your public key so someone--me--can use it to encrypt a file for you--and only you--to decrypt with that key."

3.8 EXPORTING A PUBLIC KEY

Sam points Bob to his terminal window again, and says, "There are a couple of ways to publish your public key, and by 'publish' I mean 'make available to at least one other person'. The surest way to get your key published is to send it to a public keyserver, which synchronizes with other servers. That way, keys are widely and accurately available. For practice, like we're doing now, it's not necessary to do that--you just need to get your public key to me. It could be in an e-mail, or on a web page, or in a file."

Sam continues: "The simplest is to use the `--export`[`names`] command to have GnuPG export the keys for the key names you want. Usually, it's just your own; you specify the key by the name or by e-mail address, or by the comment (remember?), or by key ID. So try it for yourself, Bob."

```
$ gpg --export bobwobble2@gmail.com
??ṕ??]???

揪???*?E??&I?py?W`?9h??E5???{?b?]?+?/????<??oi"?\?b??nVgnX#□??A?K??2??RHV?_6?;D?  ;
b??l?c`ꞟi???4?`????꓾????d_co???Xh?H?-&.`s?g]fc??ꓘA-
??uP????l?pKR`?R?kk???#??%P???Q?????S?[?G???y:?6???}??(???1C??????FE??,Hq??x?????1
*??.?F?9!????)??????r??FT_?e\R!?3??':p4<??!?m??`.?$?U???? a?P????ꞓT1???3?????*ḗ??d
徒
0;w?t?<??M7?0?%>v???(????a?Q&e???khe!??cj?4G:?M!??B?G?U?fX???g?@oe!5n?SI{???+?Iy?&
_.□?(??+?e FJ?9~=?3??9???;=?)tUxe~u??j???]z??i??w4?Ɓso???y ?$Hv????ꞋY]???iY
```

"Oh, that seems wrong. I think I need the ASCII armor now, do I not?" asks Bob. "I think I can figure it out myself. You said the options come first, and then the command, did you not, Sam? I think I have it:"

```
$ gpg -a --export bobwobble2@gmail.com

-----BEGIN PGP PUBLIC KEY BLOCK-----

mQENBFD6xdsBCADOoWUF9vpysSFFZzXuz62jEKejkejRkwzRU5eA5BA0evpDMJzi
He7S1pPSj2TjN8N4BDjFiouRaB+YND9zNxhxxuZaxC7evcdWeAV44snmSjmvokhM
a4ucE6Z9fN/crKUm8A36owFdAoyYvumeprcSwdQqjEWYzCYDSf1wed9XIuA5aLLy
qagZRTXW+8F7m2L+XeIryi/MxsT2PPMUtG9pzYyUXNdiqcEQAG4EVmeACAFuWCPu
r5ua+kHzMyp1YR1MMCZO1zKnIpx/wYzDMyyFiJl+KDBsD9AIebKM6MXSIZzudJ+Q
[and so on...]
```

"That's right, Bob," says Sam. "Copy that text block from the command line window and paste it into an e-mail to me. You've got my address on my card." As they wait for the e-mail to be delivered, Bob asks, "What was that you said about keyservers, Sam?"

Sam says, "Sending me your public key like this, by e-mail, keeps things between you and me (and the companies hosting our e-mail, and our ISPs, and whoever might be monitoring the network). Sometimes sending to a keyserver is often a better way to do it, because if Eve ('the eavesdropper') is monitoring the network, she can figure out I'm planning to exchange ciphertext with someone if I get their public key in the mail. That gives her a great reason to continue monitoring your communications. The encryption will work, but if Eve is determined and, let's say she works in a government agency, maybe she will be able to find your secrets some other way besides decrypting your ciphertexts."

Bob is getting annoyed--Mrs. Bob has always insisted on keeping tabs on Bob, and is nothing if not determined. Bob mutters "How does he know so much about me?" as Sam, oblivious, continues: "If you send your key to a keyserver, Eve has a much harder time figuring out who is going to send you a ciphertext, because she has no way of knowing who gets your public key from the server. But if she's sniffing your Internet connection, she will know you've uploaded a key to the keyserver, and she'll know your public key. Either way, if your Internet is being sniffed, encryption may attract unwanted attention."

Despite Bob's growing discomfort, Sam continues: "I guess the best way to keep things completely on the down-low is to exchange a key in person, with paper and pencil. That way, it may not be *as* obvious to Eve that you're exchanging any ciphertext with anyone, and it should be more difficult for her to figure out who the other person is."

Sam, engrossed in the discussion, is completely oblivious to Bob's agitation, until Bob interrupts: "Listen, Mr. Mallory, I would like answers right now. What is this all about?"

Sam, turning to Bob, says, "Oh, it's about using GnuPG, of course. I've got your public key now, so let me encrypt a file for you and send it back; read the file and you'll understand." Sam stands, pointing to the washroom, and says, "If you'll excuse me?"

3.9 COMMAND SUMMARY AND REVIEW

Command	Description and Notes
gpg --import [filename]	Import a key to the local keyring; where the key is stored in *filename*; an ASCII-armored key may be entered interactively.
gpg -ao filename -r recipient -e	Encrypt using the public key of *recipient* (identified by name, e-mail, a string in the comment, or by key ID). Generate ASCII-armored output to *filename*.
gpg -ar user ID -e	Encrypt using the public key of *recipient*, generating ASCII-armored output echoed to the terminal display.
gpg --key-gen	Generate a public key pair.
gpg -a --export key ID	Export the public key identified by *key ID*; output will be ASCII armored and echoed to the terminal display.

3.10 REVIEW QUESTIONS

1. How would you export a public key into a file, rather than output to the standard output (the terminal screen)?
2. What *is* really going on here? How did it happen?
3. How would you revoke a public key, knowing that this (gpg --send-keys[key ID]) is how to send a key to a keyserver?

CHAPTER 4

Public Key Functions

Sam, allowing Bob some time to ponder the implications of his new situation, expects Bob not just to understand how much trouble he's in, but also to accept that he is no longer the master of his own fate. But mostly, Sam wants Bob to allow himself the possibility of a happy ending--if he can follow instructions. To imagine that there may be a carrot hidden somewhere in this new scenario, something--anything--to motivate beyond the stick that Sam believes he now holds over Bob's head.

Sam waits for 10 minutes before returning to his seat.

"Relax, Mr. Wobble. To be sure we all understand what's going on here, why don't you tell me what you've figured out, and I'll correct you when you're wrong. OK?"

"Yes, of course." Bob responds, the image of reason. He'd realized what was happening even before Sam had stood up. "It's about using GnuPG. You sniffed me, a Sylvanian physicist in Boston for a conference, downloading software ordinarily forbidden in Sylvania. You know my wife Eve is director of Computer Technology Division for Sylvanian Security Service (SSS). Also of course, you know about my acquaintance with young girl of name Alice."

Sam nods, and asks, "And?"

"And, you are a spy. CIA, perhaps?" Bob asks, and Sam nods again as Bob wonders whether it even matters for whom Sam works.

Bob continues, "You want me to work for you, as a spy. I'm a scientist, I have information, I can get more from wife if I snoop on her. If I do not, you turn me over to SSS with proof I've written a protest essay and used cryptography, which could put me in Sylvanian prison for 20 years. As a rational person, I would not like to go to prison."

"You tricked me into turning thought crimes into actual crimes: by downloading and using GnuPG, and by writing a protest essay. I've taken risks, so, you believe it is my great good fortune to be caught by CIA, not

SSS." Bob continues: "What is going on now, I think, is you are teaching me to protect myself with GnuPG while I conduct my treasonous acts."

Sam nods once more, and Bob says, "OK, Sam, let us continue please. I'm ready."

4.1 DECRYPTING AND VERIFYING

"Check your e-mail, Bob, and you'll find that message from me I mentioned earlier; it's been encrypted with your public key, and I've signed it with *my* public key. Your task now is to decrypt the message and verify the signature. What do you do, and why?"

Bob opens his Gmail account and finds the new message from Sam. In it is an ASCII-armored block of text. Bob says: "First, I highlight and copy the message block, and," a pause, and with less certainty, "then, I decrypt, and then I verify?"

"Close," says Sam, "but it's easier than that. If a ciphertext is encrypted and signed, GnuPG decrypts and automatically verifies the signature without any extra commands. Try it; just `gpg --decrypt` and paste the message." Bob starts typing, pasting in the PGP block after entering the command:

```
$ gpg -d
-----BEGIN PGP MESSAGE-----

hQEMAzioXFcWP+2QAQgAr6I2o0KBVHAlLq2qvBkWqS8ixIM4f9mHiGEzPJySSOcO
JGlKzoPzU7dZJd5KHbZvFYB+uHXtdYgTJ6ZpAnQ9DLIspoiEwJ1PwjnuHSk63RhD
NiSOxurW3NZtemkTzFhgSBywGr2I2zIwSx8VTFVMn6YlhE4LE9kHBJKp96SYCy2K
dXVPOEtxzFj+aRrayOrh1cIWMlUdKqjZ0SrOVvMvtoN41Ghlw9d3tjNQ5hdbzTuG
zJl4NNei9oiL5NjkudnR7m4uB68mFRQGGikdq6NY0UHbe+VsQSysaIIFpFN7/pHL
RUoDK6KUZ3vuXOgSmtuBaX0/Nul6JkiRspF4RqvNqtLAzQFb+mVVwBxCtj/fKPFf
qFvd64KNKVXQXFSheZ6E0QNFhcKVS6Vbavj6c0Nfs43lgcT4XNBy+GZlFdW3pAkH
7z34LH0s9hiQjmNNbTMk+Z7YsbBZDyY4/FO8h+lAqJkTj/uqfol20eLn2HHNNMrj
2J7h4LbkfLLVjEhW/mPz5rDxvzEeEJxfmxHrgwfCMVLU5T9MKzDRxIVrC8j14kb8
nYU/8Wz0EnFPSVxsvCHzk9K6aE3mCQLsyZiy6XyClDqrKEFhyTPx+O5KWOHMIY6o
2FtnxGmgn+ACiiUpx4A+6DiSwcO16CCYTwTGiqdndOElL+mE6i9IYSQbIFcXurjo
n/13/D/mshsC2D7tBjlPaHdDpxEhXCqW2E4TB1RSJdDsX0EwSjn4bF3cqSJg08mr
YfzNEHMadsqzL6Qh7cWeU5htnREBkBWdGCM4utAwfetQm8VhdnjH4WTGND0OYOCN
7FZIbL3vohbwsfvq7+xgGlqd6vydhEDW2rO1wQigpArG00SraLd7P67Ddx/bHuE=
=fhni
-----END PGP MESSAGE-----

You need a passphrase to unlock the secret key for
user: "Bob Wobble (test #1) <bobwobble2@gmail.com>"
2048-bit RSA key, ID 163FED90, created 2013-01-21 (main key ID 84F84DD2)
```

Sam taps on Bob's laptop. "Now it might get a little messy, because you may get a dialog box prompting for a passphrase before you finish entering the ciphertext, which you've got to do by entering the 'end-of-file' sequence. So, enter the passphrase, then <Enter> and <Ctrl-d>," says Sam. "That's for OS X/Linux; on Windows it's <Enter>, then <Ctrl-z>, then <Enter> again."

"Sam, this is very annoying and complicated. Is there not an easier way?"

Sam thinks it over. "Actually, there are a couple of things you can do. You could get a plug-in for your browser or e-mail client, it will let you highlight ASCII-armored text and use a dropdown menu to decrypt or validate it. Best to look for a good one that meets your needs after you learn more about GnuPG at the command line."

Sam pauses, "The other solution it to dump the ciphertext into a file. GnuPG handles files very nicely at the command line. If you use a thumb drive and you can hide it well when you're not using it, you should be OK. But remember to securely erase anything incriminating on that drive."

"I see," said Bob, "but explain to me why this stupid dialog box keeps popping up? Why not just prompt me at the command line. It's so confusing."

4.1.1 Pinentry Dialog Box and RAM Caching

"Good question, Bob. *Pinentry* is a collection of GUI dialog programs that GnuPG uses to accept input of passphrases (and PINs, thus the name). Pinentry makes entering passphrases more secure because it is more difficult to run a brute-force attack, and you can use some versions of Pinentry to manage how long a passphrase is kept in memory."

Sam continues: "When you enter a passphrase, it *has* to go into the system's working memory[1]--there's no other way to get it from you to GnuPG. The big question is, how long will that passphrase *stay* in memory? For greater security, I want it to be forgotten immediately-- but that can be annoying and inconvenient, especially if I have several tasks to complete that require my passphrase, like encrypting or signing a bunch of different files."

---

[1]That is, the system's Random Access Memory (RAM).

"Some versions of Pinentry give me the option of specifying how long to cache a passphrase (my Linux version does this; Mac and Windows versions aren't as nice). Also, there are variables I can set in my GnuPG configuration file to change the time-to-live of the cache[2]."

"If my passphrase is cached in memory I must never walk away from a logged-in terminal session: anyone could walk up and decrypt all of my ciphertexts without entering a passphrase; if they've got software that can copy the contents of the system memory, they could even actually discover my passphrase!" Sam waits to see if Bob is getting this; then goes on, "For now, remember to close all GnuPG terminal sessions, quit out of the terminal program, and shut your computer down when you're not using it."

Bob asks, "Shut down? Power off, or can I go to hibernate or sleep mode?"

"No! Even if you lock your screen, there are ways to grab keys and passphrases out of RAM. Shut it down!" Sam says. "Bob, here's my advice":

Clear your system memory by powering down after GnuPG sessions. Unlike disk storage, system RAM is cleared out when the system is powered down. And if you use sleep mode, your system is just writing what's in RAM to a file on your disk--pretty easy to break you passphrases that way.

Use Linux. I know, Linux is supposedly more complicated, but it's also more predictable for command line issues than OS X or Windows. Also, GnuPG and related software usually works best on Linux.

Run GnuPG from a LiveBoot version of Linux. Using a "LiveBoot" version of Linux--one that boots directly from a DVD or a thumb drive[3]--and you can do what you want without leaving any trace on your system drives.

"Let's get back to work. I'll show you how to work with files."

---

[2]See "Managing shell command history in OS X/Linux" (http://crypto.loshin.com/?p=1013).
[3]See http://www.ubuntu.com/download/help/try-ubuntu-before-you-install for an example.

4.1.2 Storing ASCII-Armored Text in a File

Sam points to Bob's computer and says, "Let's work with that cipher-text block in a file. Open a text editor[4]--not a word processor--paste the ciphertext into a new file and save it with an .asc extension, try using bob.txt.asc. Then try decrypting it as a file." Bob opens TextEdit (he uses OS X) and does as Sam says, then enters the command (and passphrase when prompted):

```
$ gpg -d bob.txt.asc

You need a passphrase to unlock the secret key for
user: "Bob Wobble (test #1) <bobwobble2@gmail.com>"
2048-bit RSA key, ID 163FED90, created 2013-01-21 (main key ID 84F84DD2)

gpg: encrypted with 2048-bit RSA key, ID 163FED90, created 2013-01-21
       "Bob Wobble (test #1) <bobwobble2@gmail.com>"
Welcome to the team, Bob.
gpg: Signature made Mon Jan 21 09:47:23 2013 EST using RSA key ID 1A0F711A
gpg: Good signature from "Sam Mallory <sam.mallory.404@gmail.com>"
gpg: WARNING: This key is not certified with a trusted signature!
gpg:          There is no indication that the signature belongs to the owner.
Primary key fingerprint: 3835 6BF3 AA97 48C9 173B  DEA5 6198 1C18 5126 6592
```

Sam says, "Look what happens: first GnuPG prompts you for your passphrase to unlock your secret key (actually, private key of the public key pair); then it decrypts and outputs the message to the screen ('Welcome to the team, Bob'); then it reports a good signature from me," says Sam. "This is fine for plaintext that *is* actual *plain* text (that is, letters and numbers), but if the original file was a binary file--an image or video--you would need to write the decrypted output into a file."

Before Bob can get his question out, Sam adds, "Oh, about that warning? It's one of the coolest things about the OpenPGP protocol." Sam says as he sips amber liquid from a tumbler that has recently appeared on his tray table. Scotch, probably, thinks Bob.

4.2 WEB OF TRUST

"Back in the early days of the Internet, people did amazing things by turning traditional models upside down. Instead of using servers to host information for dumb clients, the Internet let computers interact as peers. Instead of storing databases centrally, people

---

[4]Good open source text editors include Gedit, Emacs, and Vim; versions are available for most OSes. Notepad is included with Windows; TextEdit with OS X.

started using the Internet to distribute database functions." Bob sips and continues:

"Think of each OpenPGP key pair as a record in a distributed database. Each 'record', stored on the key holder's computer, includes the public key, name and e-mail address, key ID, key creation and expiration dates, and so on. With no central authority to dispense certainty about key registrants (let's call it 'trust'), how do you trust a key holder unless you've met in person and have checked each other's picture ID?" Bob starts to think about it, but Sam goes on:

"It's one of the biggest problems with public key encryption: how do you trust the public key you're looking at belongs to the person who claims it. Am I who I say I am? Anyone can generate a key that says their name is Sam Mallory--so how can you trust me when I claim to be Sam Mallory?"

"Sam, you are getting very philosophical. What does this mean?" asks Bob.

"What it means is that instead of requiring a central certification authority of some kind, for people to register their names and public keys with, Phil Zimmermann figured back in 1992 that it would be a good idea to have individuals sign each other's keys when they have some proof of the person's identity." Sam points to the laptop again and says:

```
gpg: WARNING: This key is not certified with a trusted signature!
gpg:           There is no indication that the signature belongs to the owner.
Primary key fingerprint: 3835 6BF3 AA97 48C9 173B  DEA5 6198 1C18 5126 6592
```

"Did you see those last three lines there? The digital signature checked out, and it *says* that Sam Mallory, me, signed it--but these three lines tell you that GnuPG thinks you have no reason to believe that the 'signature belongs to the owner'."

Slamming down his drink, Sam turns to Bob and says, "Listen, right now I'm here to tell you that that *is* my public key; the fact we're sitting here having this conversation should be enough for you to trust me. So you *will* sign off on my key (which I'll show you in a minute). But for anyone else, you're going to need to check credentials like passport or drivers license, at least, before you trust the signature. Got that?"

"Sure. If *you* sign someone's public key, I should trust that key, too?" asks Bob.

"You trust it if I tell you to trust it--and don't trust any key that *hasn't* been signed by me," replies Sam. "Listen, the web of trust idea is pretty cool, it's just not really taken off in the same way that, say, Facebook has taken off with users. It's kind of like LinkedIn[5] in how it gives you access to other people's networks. But with web of trust, you're certifying how trustworthy you judge someone to be. If it's a stranger whose passport you've checked, that's one thing--but if it's your cousin or lifelong friend or long-time work buddy and you check their passport, you might give that person's key a higher level of certification; if you're confident they are serious about security, you might even trust other people who *they* trust."

"But, as cool as the web of trust is, some people never bother with it. You can still use GnuPG without thinking about web of trust--it's easy if you don't have many keys and get them mostly in person. Or else if you keep in mind that using a key you pulled off some web site may or may not be the key for the person it purports to be." Sam pauses, then says, "Just remember to be careful about who you trust, and whose keys you trust."

4.2.1 Signing a Key

Sam says, "Time to sign my key." Bob starts with `gpg -h` to see if he can figure it out. "Should I use `gpg --lsign-key` or `gpg --sign-key`?" he asks.

Sam says, "Excellent question. GnuPG help isn't very helpful here. It says `--lsign-key` is to 'sign a key locally' and `--sign-key` is 'sign a key'. The difference is that signing a key is a big deal: it means that you're announcing that you've determined the key holder is who she says she is. You're announcing, 'I trust this person's key'."

"If you weren't doing spying for us, Bob, I'd say, don't worry about it. But since you are spying for us, I'm going to suggest you stay away from making public announcements about anyone's keys. OK?" Sam continues:

"So, you use the `--lsign-key` command when you want to note that you trust a key, you just don't want to allow your signature to be

---

exported off the local computer. Regular users use that option when they have someone's key, and they think it's probably fine but they just haven't gotten around to verifying it yet. Otherwise, the `--sign-key` option is for when you're ready to take a position on someone's public key, and don't mind having your opinion propagate around the Internet."

"So, sign my key locally. There's no need for you to start emitting information about who your friends are or who you know. I know I talked about that web of trust, but in this situation you probably don't want to leave too many digital footprints."

Bob signs Sam's public key, locally. "First, I need to find your key ID, so I command GnuPG to list all my keys, and then I copy the key ID for your key":

```
$ gpg -k
/home/bob/.gnupg/pubring.gpg
----------------------------
pub   2048R/84F84DD2 2013-01-21 [expires: 2013-01-25]
uid                  Bob Wobble (test #1) <bobwobble2@gmail.com>
sub   2048R/163FED90 2013-01-21 [expires: 2013-01-25]

pub   2048R/1A0F711A 2013-01-15 [expires: 2015-07-04]
uid                  Sam Mallory <sam.mallory.404@gmail.com>
sub   2048R/DDBB6A4D 2013-01-15 [expires: 2015-07-04]
```

Sam points to the short list and says, "You've only got two keys in your keyring, so it's not a big deal, but you could also command GnuPG to list keys that match 'Sam', by using the command `gpg -k Sam`." Bob tries it, and says, "That's good to know. Does that trick work for other commands?"

"GnuPG is pretty good about letting you specify what you want. So if you want to list out keys or fingerprints, you can specify a string that should be in the name or e-mail address. For instance, if you want to see all keys that have 'gmail' in them, you can do that," says Sam. "You can also specify more than one key ID in a single command. So what next?"

Bob says, "I have your key ID, now I want to sign it, locally, so:"

```
$ gpg --lsign-key 1A0F711A
```

"And GnuPG lists out all this information about the key I want to sign, to make sure":

```
pub  2048R/1A0F711A  created: 2013-01-15  expires: 2015-07-04  usage: SC
                     trust: unknown       validity: unknown
sub  2048R/DDBB6A4D  created: 2013-01-15  expires: 2015-07-04  usage: E
[ unknown] (1). Sam Mallory <sam.mallory.404@gmail.com>


pub  2048R/1A0F711A  created: 2013-01-15  expires: 2015-07-04  usage: SC
                     trust: unknown       validity: unknown
 Primary key fingerprint: 3E2E 4BB0 6F8C C405 6AD0  D125 3B3B B3B3 1A0F 711A

     Sam Mallory <sam.mallory.404@gmail.com>

This key is due to expire on 2015-07-04.
Are you sure that you want to sign this key with your
key "Bob Wobble (test #1) <bobwobble2@gmail.com>" (84F84DD2)

The signature will be marked as non-exportable.

Really sign? (y/N) y
```

"I enter y to 'really' sign the key," says Bob, "and, voila":

```
You need a passphrase to unlock the secret key for
user: "Bob Wobble (test #1) <bobwobble2@gmail.com>"
2048-bit RSA key, ID 84F84DD2, created 2013-01-21
```

"So I enter my passphrase, and. . ." Bob enters his passphrase in the pinentry dialog box, ". . .and, I'm back to the command prompt. Do I have to list my keys to see what happened and check that the signature is there?"

"No, actually, listing the keys won't show you the signatures on the keys." Sam says, "There's a different command to list key signatures. . ."

Bob, scanning the GnuPG help listing again, finds it: "--list-sigs, right?"

Sam says, "Right. And that's one of the commands that gives you the option to specify a particular key you want, or that will give you information on *all* your keys if you leave the key ID out. For one key, enter the command with the key ID you want to see."

"Do I need to use that prefix for the key ID? You know, the 0x before the key ID number?" Bob asks.

"No, you don't need to do that; you can also use a user name or e-mail address," answers Sam, as Bob complies:

```
$ gpg --list-sigs 1A0F711A
gpg: checking the trustdb
gpg: no ultimately trusted keys found
pub   2048R/1A0F711A 2013-01-15 [expires: 2015-07-04]
uid                  Sam Mallory <sam.mallory.404@gmail.com>
sig 3        1A0F711A 2013-01-15  Sam Mallory <sam.mallory.404@gmail.com>
sig  L       84F84DD2 2013-01-23  Bob Wobble (test #1) <bobwobble2@gmail.com>
sub   2048R/DDBB6A4D 2013-01-15 [expires: 2015-07-04]
sig          1A0F711A 2013-01-15  Sam Mallory <sam.mallory.404@gmail.com>
```

"Your signature shows up on my key now," says Sam. "See that letter L there? That's to remind you that your signature on my key is local. The number 3 on the line above it is part of my own signature on my own key, 3 means fully trusted[6]. By default, GnuPG signs your own key when you create it, for security: if you *didn't* sign your own key, someone else could put a signature that looks like yours but is actually their own, and that's how someone could hijack *your* key. But that shouldn't ever happen these days, as GnuPG automatically signs your key for you when you generate it."

4.3 ENCRYPT AND SIGN

Sam asks, "Bob, how about you encrypt and sign a binary file to send to me? Do you have any pictures from your trip you'd like to share?" asks Sam.

"How about a photo of the secret biology lab I was shown when I visited Menotomy University? I tell GnuPG to encrypt and sign file bio_lab.jpg, for recipient 'Sam Mallory'. Do I need to specify an output file?" Bob asks.

"You can specify an output filename if you like, but by default the encrypted file will be the plaintext file plus the extension.gpg; that's for binary files. For ASCII-armored ones, the default extension is. asc," says Sam. He adds, "Oh, and you'll probably forget this, but if you encrypt files in other directories and you want to specify an output file, you've got to specify the entire filename plus directory path. If you don't, the output file gets written to whatever directory you're currently working in--not the same directory where the plaintext file is.

---

[6]See "GnuPG Signature Flags" at http://crypto.loshin.com/?p=987 for more details.

So using the default file naming option might be a good thing, most of the time."

Bob starts typing:

```
$ gpg -r 'Sam Mallory' -se bio_lab.jpg
```

Sam stops Bob before he hits <Enter>: "That will work fine, also using the key ID would be a good idea, just in case you had more than one key for me. Like this":

```
$ gpg -r ddbb6a4d -se bio_lab.jpg
```

"They're both ways to tell GnuPG to sign and encrypt the file `bio_-lab.jpg` for recipient 'Sam Mallory' (key ID `ddbb6a4d`); then, when it finishes, you can check the directory (use `ls -l bio_lab.*` command to get a listing in OS X or Linux, `dir bio_lab.*` for Windows) to see listings for plaintext and ciphertext versions of that file."

Bob says, "I can encrypt and decrypt, even sign things. I understand how to use the options. If an option needs a value, like the `--recipient` option, I need a key ID or other identifier; if `--output` option, I need a filename."

Sam, nodding, says, "Now, send me the file, and I'll decrypt and verify it, and we can talk about what digital signatures are good for."

4.4 BENEFITS OF DIGITAL SIGNATURES

Sam says, "We expect you to exercise extreme caution when communicating: authenticating our messages, and making sure your messages are verifiable."

"But why? Isn't it enough to get a message encrypted with your own key, which you gave to me personally?" asks Bob. "What does signing it do?"

"Digital signature does three things: first, it identifies *you* as the person who signed the message: that's *authentication*. Second, it guarantees that the message I receive is the same message you signed, unmodified in transit: that's *integrity*. Third, having signed a plaintext, that signature is an undeniable proof: you cannot deny you signed it. That's *non-repudiation.*" Sam recites. "When we send you instructions, you'll probably be interested to know whether *we* sent them or someone less agreeable. Likewise, you'll want to know the instructions you've received are complete and unchanged in any way from what we sent."

"So, how am I going to use signatures, then?" asks Bob.

Sam answers, slowly: "When you send me a message, encrypt and sign it. When you send me a file, encrypt and sign it. When I send you a file or message, decrypt it and verify the signature. Verify it means being certain to read the messages that GnuPG returns after it decrypts."

"OK," says Bob, with a hint of uncertainty. "That seems simple?"

Sam, noting Bob's uncertainty, says, "Yes, it *seems* simple, and it *is* simple, if you follow the rules. We're going to set up a cover story for you, in case you are discovered passing encrypted messages back and forth between the United States and Sylvania, so you won't automatically be considered a traitor, especially by your wife. We'll also set up some *duress codes* for you, so if you're detected you can signal me without tipping off the SSS--or your wife."

"Cover story?" asks Bob.

"Yes," Sam says: "Yours will be that you're carrying on with Alice, that sweet graduate student at Menotomy University. It doesn't matter that you feel only innocent, paternal feelings toward her. Would you rather your wife suspect you of being an old fool and committing adultery or that you're a traitor?"

Bob nods, unhappily. He'd rather not be suspected of anything, but that train has left the station. Sam continues:

"A duress code is something you say or do that isn't obvious, but that signals you can no longer trust that your message is secure. It might be as simple as including a certain word in every message, and omitting that word when security has been breached. For instance, you might start normal messages with 'Dear Alice', but use something else, like, 'Hi cupcake!' if your activities are exposed. It could be even more subtle, like using different punctuation or a misspelled word. We'll work out the details before we land, don't worry about that. Meanwhile, let's take a little break--it's time for lunch!" With that, a flight attendant arrives to ask the two whether they would prefer steak or lobster--or both.

Bob sips his drink and clicks a link to a cat video his wife "Liked" on Facebook. "Oh what a silly kitty, that's your own tail!" Bob thinks to himself, "And perhaps there is a way out of this situation that doesn't end with bread and water and a cell for me." Bob opens a message window, and begins composing to his wife:

Dearest cupcakes: Am having great flight, all praise to the Leader. What an adorable kitty! You know how much I love cats! Cannot wait to see our kitty Walter--if only you could bring him to the airport when you come to get me.

"I wonder if Sam knows I'm allergic to cats," Bob ponders, as he clicks "Send."

4.5 COMMAND SUMMARY AND REVIEW

Command	Description and Notes
`gpg --decrypt [filename]` `gpg -d [filename]`	Decrypt *filename*.
`gpg --lsign-key key ID`	Sign *key ID*, but for local use only; do not export the signature on the key.
`gpg --sign-key key ID`	Sign *key ID*, and allow that signature to be exported to a keyserver.
`gpg --list-keys [key ID]` `gpg -k [key ID]`	List key information about *key ID*; if no key ID is specified, list all keys on the keyring.
`gpg --list-sigs key ID`	List all signatures on the *key ID* specified.
`gpg --recipient key ID -se [filename]`	Encrypt and sign *filename* for the recipient specified by the *key ID*.

4.6 REVIEW QUESTIONS

1. What proof of identity has Sam Mallory offered to Bob? Should Bob trust him?
2. Make a list of all the GnuPG commands and options that Bob has learned so far.
3. *Web of trust* is one way to distribute trust in public keys; see how it differs from the other option, *certificate authority*. Which is more commonly used? Why?
4. In what ways could Bob's message be modified to contain impromptu duress codes?

CHAPTER 5

More About Signatures

"Explain to me again what a signature actually is. Because when I sign a file, the output seems to be encrypted, not just signed," says Bob as the conversation turns back to cryptography. Though Sam's earlier comments about Alice bother him, Bob knows better than to let it get to him, at least not yet.

"One thing to remember," says Sam, "GnuPG gives you three ways to sign, and two of those produce what looks like encrypted output."

5.1 "DECRYPTING" A DIGITAL SIGNATURE

Sam says: "Consider GnuPG's roots as a tool for facilitating communication in the early Internet, and it's obvious why GnuPG compresses output. That's what you did when generating files transmitted over a network back in 1991 or so, because networks were slower back then[1]. The compressed file *looks* as if it's ciphertext, but it's just compressed-- and easily uncompressed into plaintext that a human can recognize or an application program can open." Sam pauses, and says, "Decrypt a signed file, and GnuPG extracts the original file--and lets you know it was signed, though it can only verify the signature if you've got the signer's public key. See?"

```
$ gpg --output testing.txt --decrypt testing.txt.gpg
gpg: Signature made Mon Jan 28 10:49:16 2013 EST using RSA key ID C81BDD7F
gpg: Can't check signature: public key not found
```

"This is a typical GnuPG behavior: it looks as if nothing happened, maybe even an error that prevented anything from happening. But the gpg: messages tell me testing.txt.gpg was signed by someone whose key I don't have, so the signature can't be checked. I can still extract the plaintext (use the --output option to save a file) by commanding GnuPG to decrypt. The output file testing.txt holds

---

[1]Actually, it's more to do with bandwidth, which is the carrying capacity of a network, but the point being that smaller files are easier to send over any network, and require less storage, so compression is a standard function for many networking tools.

the 'decrypted' plaintext that GnuPG *uncompressed* from the original 'ciphertext' file."

5.2 MORE ABOUT SIGNATURES

Sam explains: "When signing, the first thing GnuPG calculates is the signature itself, on the original data. Next, it *compresses* the data along with the signature. So if you have a text file with 1,000 lines repeating the same message ('this is a test'), your plaintext file will be 16,000 bytes but the signed output file will only be a few hundred bytes. That's because right after signing, GnuPG compresses the whole thing (original data file + signature data)."

Sam continues: "The signature is done on the original plaintext, because *that* is what is being signed--the signature is meant to be proof that the public key owner created or approved the data being signed. Compression is done after that, so if the signed file will also be encrypted there is less to encrypt. If it's not encrypted, the compressed file is still easier to handle (less data to download or process)."

"If you wanted to, you could probably have GnuPG encrypt something and *then* sign it, but that's not usually a good idea. Signing before encrypting means the signature is also encrypted, keeping details about the source of the data (who signed it) private. If you compress *after* encrypting, the file, which will already be mostly random-seeming data, won't compress very much if at all."

Bob asks, "But that seems to make things difficult--what about signing a message in e-mail? Is there some way to sign something without turning it into ciphertext?"

"Yes, and that's why there are *three* different types of GnuPG signatures," says Sam, "not just one or two."

5.3 DIGITAL SIGNATURE TYPES

"When signing data, GnuPG takes input (a file or chunk of text) as a single unit, then signs it. That is, it generates a hash on the data to be signed and then generates the digital signature, and then adds the signature to a copy of the original data. It's like wrapping a package: you can't see the inside without taking the wrapping paper off. After generating the signature, GnuPG takes the signed data, plus the signature, and compresses it. *That's* like taking the wrapped package and putting it inside *another* box. And then, GnuPG takes the signed and compressed data, and encrypts it--like taking the whole thing and putting it inside a locked container."

Sam continues: "The default type of signature is called an *attached signature*, and the 'signature' is actually a file (or block of data) that contains the cryptographic data generated when signing the plaintext *plus* the plaintext. This is what you get when you use the basic GnuPG command gpg --sign."

"The only way to get any data out of the signature itself is to 'verify' the file--but that is done by extracting the plaintext after verifying the signature, and extracting the compressed data prior to verifying. And you can verify two ways, first, with the gpg --verify command, which reports back on whether the signature is good or not (or with an error if the file being verified isn't recognized as a signed file). Second, GnuPG will verify as well as decrypt the file if you use the gpg --decrypt command."

"As you say, Bob, this *is* a pain: the obvious difficulty is that a signed plaintext file becomes a file that is, if not encrypted, no longer accessible as plaintext. You must extract the plaintext before you can see what's been signed."

Sam continues: "Two problems with default GnuPG signatures are, first, how to validate downloaded files without forcing all downloaders to extract the desired file from a signature file. The second is how to generate ASCII-armored output to include signed plaintexts in e-mails or other text-oriented applications."

"Wrapping plaintext with the signature means that the signed file, if it's a program or application data, has to be extracted to be used, and thus is no longer the 'same' file as signed[2]." Sam pushes his plate away and goes on:

"So, three types of signatures are supported in GnuPG: *clearsigned signatures*, *detached signatures*, and *attached signatures*. To generate

---

[2]The extracted plaintext file's contents will be the same as the original plaintext, but the file's metadata (e.g., the date it was created) will be different. It's a minor issue, but still an issue.

ASCII-armored output, without any compression, use `gpg --clearsign`. For example, I can clearsign a quick message to my mom[3], and it will look like this:"

```
-----BEGIN PGP SIGNED MESSAGE-----
Hash: SHA1

Hi Mom! On my way to Sylvania, on schedule!
-----BEGIN PGP SIGNATURE-----

iQEcBAEBAgAGBQJRBqciAAoJEO8+juPIG91/ffIH/Rbs9IVOIEpJYVInMYZw/EMt
is9HL4wwNWE9Qw1VKv4hXpB8XBID9Uub7xR1QWhtQ0D+ukLyC6ur+nLqLIVcZUJc
5wOVBYvdjCeBgV7Go+QRgChVapBKBZyTJuahE6PgtXh1c3nekHCcXsencs6azTTG
qTMTxm7bjEEE1G3y1NL85hEOdA2A/LIBjz3btv18Cp3vLz78/av2StMdDt5DiSdg
NB10hQMSEzPi5h8I3fNIGdFtOMHWBGRFIjs74G7GrLsA6P9dbU+B/8uKCMFEBqD3
1b9Ze4yuey7BaWQHsBj7ZTtg7tOmRvZuFVS9tbIfrKBkrDUVdwoq4GDyuxDH2Mw=
=/hbp
-----END PGP SIGNATURE-----
```

"I can copy that whole thing into an e-mail message, or even take a picture of it and send the picture--as long as the whole thing is entered back into GnuPG and verified." Sam says, "My mother doesn't *have* to verify the text to read it, but if she wants to be certain it was I who sent it, she can verify it at her leisure."

"With detached signatures you can access plaintext without verification, but more often used to sign downloaded files, especially software. For example, when you download GnuPG, you download a separate signature file. If you're not worried about integrity of the program, you can use it without verification--or if you are worried, you can use the detached signature to verify the file without changing the downloaded file[4]. This is how to do a detached signature on a file":

```
$ gpg --detach-sign linuxdistro.iso

You need a passphrase to unlock the secret key for
user: "Sam Mallory <sam.mallory.404@gmail.com>"
2048-bit RSA key, ID C81BDD7F, created 2012-11-12

$ ls -l *.iso*
-rw-r--r--  1 sam.mallory  staff  13094912 Jan 30 17:06 linuxdistro.iso
-rw-r--r--  1 sam.mallory  staff       287 Jan 30 17:07 linuxdistro.iso.sig
```

---

[3]Sam uses the command `gpg --clearsign` and enters his message interactively. The output shown is displayed on the terminal screen, and can be copied and pasted into a message.
[4]You should verify *all* downloads, *especially* if the download relates to security.

"It's a typical GnuPG command: `--detach-sign` (abbreviated as `-b`). GnuPG signs the thing after the command (in this case, the file `linuxdistro.iso`, though it could also be a block of text you enter interactively[5]), and outputs to a file called `linuxdistro.iso.sig` (default: the signed filename plus `.sig`)."

Sam continues: "GnuPG generates the detached signature, but instead of writing it out as GnuPG output file (which implies compression, by the way), GnuPG writes signature data into a small separate file. You can't authenticate the signature without both the original file and the `.sig` file. To verify the detached signature, put both files in the same directory and use the `--verify` command":

```
$ gpg --verify linuxdistro.iso.sig
gpg: Signature made Tue Jan 29 10:55:36 2013 EST using RSA key ID C81BDD7F
gpg: Good signature from "Sam Mallory <sam.mallory.404@gmail.com>"
```

"Could I use the `--decrypt` command too?" asks Bob.

"Yes, but if you're not sure what's in a GnuPG file[6], just run GnuPG without specifying a command; for more information about what happens, use the `-v` (verbose) option," says Sam, "and add v's for more verbosity (e.g., `-vvv`)."

"OK," Bob says, "Now, tell me about verifying the different kinds of signatures."

5.4 SIGNING AND VERIFYING, SUMMARIZED

"I have been giving examples along the way, but here it is all in one place," replies Sam as he hands Bob a printed page, "And for good measure, also a summary of how to sign things."

---

[5]Not something you would do often; to do it, use `gpg -ab`, save the block of text into a file (e.g., `example.txt`), and paste the resulting ASCII-armored signature into a file too (e.g., `example.txt.sig`). There are other ways to do this using the `--output` option.

[6]GnuPG files are identified by their extensions; most common are: `*.asc` for ASCII-armored output, `*.gpg` for binary output ciphertext, and `*.sig` for detached signatures.

Command	Description and Notes
gpg --sign *filename* gpg -s *filename*	Digitally sign *filename* and save the signed file as *filename.* *gpg.* Common options include ASCII armor, specifying a different filename; a block of text can be signed interactively (no filename entered at command line).
gpg --detach-sign *filename* gpg -b *filename*	Digitally sign *filename* and save the signature in a separate file named *filename.sig* (leaving *filename* untouched). Common options include ASCII armor, specifying a different filename; a block of text can be signed interactively (no filename entered at command line).
gpg --clearsign *filename*	Digitally sign *filename* and output to the default file (*filename.asc*) containing the original text plus ASCII- armored signature. Done interactively on a block of text, the clearsigned data is output on screen (unless an output filename is specified).
gpg --verify *filename*	Verifies *filename* if a valid signature file; returns signature information only.
gpg --verify *filename* signature	Verifies a detached file (*filename*) with the detached signature (*signature*); returns signature information only.
gpg --verify	For interactive verification of a clearsigned block of text, or ASCII-armored attached signature block.
gpg --decrypt *filename*	Plaintext is output to the screen.
gpg -o filename1 -d *filename2*	Decrypt *filename2* and output (save) as *filename1.*
Note: Default filenames are noted above, but signatures and plaintext can be written to nondefault filenames using the --*output* filename option.	

5.4.1 Verifying a Digitally Signed File (Attached Signature)

Sam says, "Most digital signatures I see are digitally signed text blocks in e-mail or newsgroups, and digitally signed downloaded files with detached signatures—but the simplest to verify is a digitally signed file with attached signature."

"An attached digital signature may make verification easier, but it also makes verification mandatory to use the file or data. Detached signatures (for files) or ASCII armoring (for text messages) allow the files or data to be used without verification." Sam goes on, "To verify an attached digital signature, you can use the raw GnuPG command, and it should verify and write a plaintext file":

```
$ gpg example.txt.gpg
gpg: Signature made Thu Dec 13 13:33:42 2012 EST using RSA key ID C81BDD7F
gpg: Good signature from "Peter Loshin (Practical Cryptography 2012 -2014) "
```

"GnuPG identifies that the file specified in the command, example.txt.gpg, contains a signature for a file called example. txt; that file is automatically extracted into the same directory as the signature file." Sam continues: "To verify the file without extracting it":

```
gpg --verify example.txt.gpg
```

"and to output the file to a different filename from the original":

```
gpg --output my_example.txt example.txt.gpg
```

"And by the way, Bob, that was an adorable message you sent to your wife," Sam says, watching Bob carefully.

Bob, looking surprised, says, "I would have e-mailed her from the airport, but I was preoccupied, so I thought it would be alright. Is it a problem? She expects always to be notified when I board my flight. I did not think you would mind."

Satisfied with Bob's response, Sam says, "No problem--your message arrives soon in Eve's mailbox. I like cats, too. Will she actually bring Walter to the airport?"

"She might, Sam; if she does you will find him to be quite adorable," answers Bob. "You are monitoring my Internet activity through your wi-fi hotspot, correct? It means I cannot keep my data private from you, I suppose."

"You suppose correctly, Bob," says Sam, "You know, 'Trust, but verify'."

"I will be very careful in that regard, then, Sam," says Bob as he nods, to himself.

5.5 REVIEW QUESTIONS

1. What are the three different types of GnuPG digital signatures? Why are there different types?
2. What does GnuPG do when a filename is listed and no command is specified?
3. When signing and encrypting, in what order are things done? What about compression? Is it *always* that way?
4. What are three filename extensions that identify a file as being output from GnuPG?
5. What do you think Bob and Eve's cat "Walter" is like?

CHAPTER 6

Working with Public Keys

"Sam, it seems I should have some better way to find a person's public key. And how can I be sure a public key belongs to the person I *think* it belongs to?" asks Bob. "And, you said something earlier about revoking keys. . . ."

"All excellent questions," Sam replies. "Because you will be working with keys now, you should know more including using public keyservers, revoking keys, editing keys, and most important, deciding whether or not to trust a key. We'll get to all those things in good time; first, let's talk about trusting a public key."

6.1 TRUSTING A PUBLIC KEY

Sam says: "'Trust but verify' also applies to public keys. For example, consider keyservers: they are public servers hosting user-generated content. Just because a public key has been uploaded to the keyserver doesn't mean it's true: I can upload a key with your name and your e-mail address on it, but it doesn't prove *that* key is *your* key. But, there are other ways to gain confidence."

Bob asks, "What about giving me your key directly, shouldn't I trust that?"

"That is one way to do it, but you still need to verify the key is what I say it is," replies Sam. "The obvious way is to examine the entire public key and make sure it's exactly correct--because a public key has to be exactly correct. Change one character of a public key, and that key is no longer usable."

Bob asks, "Could I print out your public key and compare it to . . . what would I compare it to?"

"First off, keep in mind that the public key you just created seems relatively short only because it has not been signed by anyone but you;

the public key block for a key that's been signed (see web of trust) is too large for a person to verify by hand," Sam says.

"If I give you my pubic key in person, and I've also posted my public key on a web site, you could compare those two keys," replies Sam, "but you'd still have to trust that I am who I say I am; most people would check my passport or drivers license in addition to my public key."

"You could also use a trusted third party, like if there were someone we both knew, and that person gave you a copy of my public key, you could compare the key I give you to the key that other person gives you--this is web of trust stuff again. This comes up with signing keys for open source projects: you download the signing key from the project web site, as well as from any mirror sites, and compare the keys from all those sources," says Sam. "But there's a better way."

6.1.1 Using Fingerprints

"The public key block is right at the edge of manageability for a person (see the one on page 26): it's a page or so (or more) of random-seeming text, which is a lot of random-seeming text for a person to process. But if you generate a secure hash on the entire public key, you have a *fingerprint* uniquely identifying the key. If I give you my public key and that key's fingerprint, you import the public key and compare fingerprints. If they match, the public key is verified."

"But it could still be fake, right?" asks Bob.

"Well, at some point you have to be willing to trust people you're encrypting data with. I can claim to be Barack Obama, e-mail address barry@whitehouse.gov, and my fingerprint checks out with a public key you found on a keyserver--but that doesn't make me the president." Sam continues: "What it *does* do is give you confidence that when you encrypt a message to me, 'Barry', *I* will be the only one who can decrypt it."

"I could show you a passport and ID to prove my identity--but since you already know I'm a spy, you probably won't trust my documents. You can, however, be confident that my public key is connected to me, the person sitting next to you, the person you know as 'Sam Mallory'. It's subtle, but it's there and you need to deal with it."

6.1.2 Other Ways of Verifying a Public Key

Sam continues: "In addition to the technical ways of verifying public keys, I try to use common sense to determine how much I need to worry."

"For example, I look for multiple sources for a public key: a book, a web site, a keyserver, wherever a public key might be published. An attacker might be able to switch out the legitimate public key on my web site, but it's harder to replace a key on a printed page in a library book. Some people even put their fingerprints on their business cards, to make things simple," says Sam.

"How do I find the fingerprint?" asks Bob, "and what actually *is* it?"

6.1.3 Fingerprints

"The fingerprint for a GnuPG public key is 40 characters, usually displayed as 10 four-character 'words'. To see a fingerprint, use the --fingerprint command":

```
gpg --fingerprint [keyID]
```

"Where [keyID][1] is the actual key ID or a partial/complete string of the key's user name or e-mail address or comment. You should also know that the key ID is the last 8 bytes of the fingerprint[2], so if you have the fingerprint handy, you also have the key ID. I can display the fingerprint of any key on my keyring by specifying that 8-byte key ID; here's mine":

```
$ gpg --fingerprint  1A0F711A
pub    2048R/1A0F711A 2013-01-15 [expires: 2015-07-04]
       Key fingerprint = 3E2E 4BB0 6F8C C405 6AD0  D125 3B3B B3B3 1A0F 711A
uid                    Sam Mallory <sam.mallory.404@gmail.com>
sub    2048R/DDBB6A4D 2013-01-15 [expires: 2015-07-04]
```

"Also, my name would work," adds Sam, "or my e-mail address, or a string from my key comment, though usually it's best to use the key ID, since it's most likely to be unambiguous--I may have more than one public key, or you may have public keys from two people with the same name, but key IDs should be unique."

Bob frowns and asks, "Should be? Are fingerprints not unique?"

---

[1]Key ID here is optional, if left off, GnuPG returns fingerprints for *all* keys on your keyring.
[2]The last 8 bytes of the fingerprint form the *short key ID*, the last 16 bytes are the long key ID.

"Well, key IDs and fingerprints can collide in theory, but in practice you shouldn't have to worry about it, at least not for now[3], " answers Sam, continuing:

"You verify the public key by comparing the fingerprint GnuPG shows to the fingerprint you get from the keyholder: look at the back of my business card, and compare to what GnuPG returns. Should be the same."

Bob taps in the command, and Sam continues: "If they don't put their fingerprint on their business cards, people may post their fingerprint online with their public key; ideally, you want to get a fingerprint directly from the keyholder (along with photo ID), or if you know the keyholder well enough to identify them over a phone connection, that's another way to get a fingerprint that you can trust."

Bob asks, "What about sending a fingerprint by e-mail?" Sam replies, "That's not a good idea because you might be tricked by a *man-in-the-middle attack*. That's where someone intercepts messages intended for you, and changes them. Even if the fingerprint is sent encrypted to your public key, that proves nothing about who is sending the message. Just remember that it's best to do verification in person."

"What about keyservers, Sam? Can't I get all this stuff from them?" asks Bob.

6.2 USING KEYSERVERS

"With keyservers, as with everything on the Internet, you should trust but verify: a keyserver is no more trustworthy than the keys submitted. Remember what I said earlier? I can upload a public key in the name of Barack Obama--or anyone--to a keyserver; that *still* doesn't make me the president." Sam continues:

"A keyserver is an Internet server that stores public keys, and responds to requests relating to public keys: you can upload a key,

---

[3]A *collision* happens when two different public keys have the same key ID; people have demonstrated methods of generating key ID collisions in OpenPGP keys, so careful users prefer the "long" 16-byte key IDs. Fingerprint collisions, while theoretically possible, have not yet been demonstrated to be practical. See http://www.asheesh.org/note/debian/short-key-ids-are-bad-news.html

download a key, or search for keys that match a name, e-mail address, or some other string. The preferred way to get to a good keyserver is to specify `keys.gnupg.net`[4]; it shouldn't matter which one you use because they are designed to synchronize with other keyservers[5]; if you update a key on one, eventually all of them that are synchronizing properly will be updated."

"For the casual user, or for the user who wants to maintain a low profile (that's you, Bob), it's not too important to worry about keyservers. They're a convenient way to publish a key, and (usually) no need to validate the information connected to your key. Think of it like Facebook for public keys."

Bob, clearly not satisfied, asks, "But how would I use a keyserver if I needed to?"

"I ask you to send me a secret using key ID `C93138D9`, but I can't give you the whole key. Instead, I give you the fingerprint and tell you to get the key from a keyserver. The least technical way to do it is to connect to the server with my browser, use the interface to search for public keys matching that ID, and then verify the fingerprint. To search on key ID, you need to prefix the ID with the characters `0x` (the numeral zero plus the lower case letter x), which identifies the rest of the value you enter as a key ID[6]."

Bob frowns again, saying, "Sam, I must protest, this seems terribly complicated."

"Or, you can use GnuPG commands to interact with keyservers; some people just like using a web interface, even if it is complicated. Keep in mind, sometimes the command line doesn't work, though

---

[4]This is the default value set in the GnuPG configuration file, `gpg.conf`, but you may enter a particular keyserver if desired.

[5]The software many keyservers run is called SKS ("Synchronizing Key Server"), and GnuPG's default keyserver, `keys.gnupg.net`, is an alias for `pool.sks-keyservers.net` which is a pool of keyservers that are active, are updated to the required minimum version of the software, and that are correctly synchronizing with the rest of the network to update keys. For more about keyservers, see `http://crypto.loshin.com/?p=1025`.

[6]Actually, it identifies the key ID you enter as a *hexadecimal* value, meaning it is a number in base 16 containing the numerals 0 through 9 plus the letters A through F which represent the numbers 10 through 16. Don't worry too much about it, just don't forget to use the prefix when searching on a keyserver.

when it does, it's great. Here's a summary of how to use keyservers at the command line," Sam says, handing a page to Bob:

Command	Notes
gpg[--keyserver *keyserver*] --send-keys *[key ID]*	Key ID prefixed with "0x" to indicate hex. Key ID is optional; leave out to send entire keyring to keyserver.
gpg[--keyserver *keyserver*] --recv-keys *key ID*	Key ID prefixed with "0x" to indicate hex.
gpg[--keyserver *keyserver*] --search-keys *search term*	Search by key ID (prefixed with "0x") or string.
gpg[--keyserver *keyserver*] --refresh-keys *[search term]*	Search term can be key ID or string; if left out, updates entire keyring. Used to check for new sigs and revocations.
Command format:	
gpg[--keyserver *keyserver*] --send-keys *key ID*	
Examples:	
gpg --keyserver keys.gnupg.net --send-keys 0xCFD7010E	
gpg --search-keys "Wobble"	
gpg --keyserver spies.example.net --refresh-keys[a]	

[a]*Note the keyserver specified: anyone can set up a keyserver and they don't have to synchronize with the rest of the OpenPGP world. In this case,* "spies.example.net" *is for spies.*

"The default keyserver is set to keys.gnupg.net in the GnuPG config file[7]," Sam notes, "but the [server name] option is available to specify a particular keyserver to use; for example, if there is some private keyserver you want to use that isn't included in the 'public' OpenPGP universe."

"If you're sending or receiving specific keys, you need to specify a key ID--using a string from the keyholder info won't work," Sam points out, "but you can use a string for searching on a keyserver, and if there are multiple hits, you'll be prompted to specify which one you want and GnuPG retrieves that one for you."

"A couple more things: with --refresh-keys, the search term is optional; if you leave it out, GnuPG will update your entire keyring from the keyserver. And with --send-keys, if you leave the search term out, GnuPG sends your entire keyring to the keyserver."

---

[7]This file is called gpg.conf and should be located in the GnuPG installation directory.

"Bob, I can search for your last name in the `keys.gnupg.net` like this":

```
$ gpg --search-keys "wobble"
```

"You've got to give `--search-keys` something to search on: a key ID, or a string[8]. If it's a string, the keyserver returns any public key with that string in the name, e-mail address, or comment. If it's a key ID, remember to prefix it with `0x`. This will return all the keys that match the string 'Wobble', like this":

```
gpg: searching for "wobble" from hkp server keys.gnupg.net
(1)     Bob Wobble <bobwobble@gmail.com>
          2048 bit RSA key 51266592, created: 2013-01-19
(2)     Wabble <wobble@freedom.net>
          1024 bit DSA key 085B3945, created: 2001-04-17
(3)     Weeble Wobble <MrWobble@MailOps.Com>
        Weeble Wobble <MrWobble@pop3free.com>
          2048 bit RSA key 6832BA53, created: 2001-02-26
(4)     Weeble Wobble <MrWobble@ic24.net>
        Weeble Wobble <MrWobble@MailOps.com>
        Weeble Wobble <MrWobble@pop3free.com>
          1024 bit DSA key 4CDEBCDE, created: 2001-02-23
(5)     Wibblers Wobble <wibbler@wobble.woo>
          1024 bit DSA key 056A54C1, created: 1999-09-27
Keys 1-5 of 5 for "wobble".  Enter number(s), N)ext, or Q)uit >
```

"Hm, Bob, it seems you've exported your key to the keyserver. How did you manage to do that..." Sam, seeing Bob's key on the list of public keys registered on a public keyserver, freaks out, but Bob sees the key and explains:

"Oh, you think that is me, but no--I told you, 'Wobble' is a common name in Sylvania; also, 'Bob'. *This* Bob Wobble is Chairman of Sylvania Freedom Party. Also known as 'Great Leader'. That is interesting, that our GL uses PGP. Also, different e-mail from mine," says Bob.

"Oh, right. *Bob* Wobble. Of course I know who that is. But see here, look up any name: 'George Bush' or 'Barack Obama' or even 'Adolph Hitler' and you'll see someone registered a public key. Means nothing--it demonstrates how little you should trust public keys you find on a keyserver, unless you have a fingerprint directly from the keyholder (or are willing to trust the signatures on the key)," says

---

[8]The string should be a complete e-mail address, or a complete name: a search on "wobbl" will fail, while "wobble" will return a selection of matches.

Sam. "Anyway, GnuPG lists all the matches it gets from the keyserver, and lets you choose which one you wanted to import; you enter the number, say '2', and hit enter, and voila":

```
gpg: requesting key 085B3945 from hkp server keys.gnupg.net
gpg: key 085B3945: public key "Wabble <wobble@freedom.net>" imported
gpg: Total number processed: 1
gpg:               imported: 1
```

"If you picked a key already on your keyring, GnuPG checks to see if the key has been updated in anyway (revocation, or additional key signings, or any other changes), and gives you a message like this if there's no change:

```
gpg: requesting key 085B3945 from hkp server keys.gnupg.net
gpg: key 085B3945: public key "Wabble <wobble@freedom.net>" not changed
gpg: Total number processed: 1
gpg:              unchanged: 1
```

"If the key has been updated, when you run `--recv-keys` your copy of the key will be updated from the keyserver:

```
$ gpg --recv-keys 0xCFD7010E
gpg: requesting key CFD7010E from hkp server keys.gnupg.net
gpg: key CFD7010E: "Neb Bebble (science) <neb@example. net>" 1 new signature
gpg: 3 marginal(s) needed, 1 complete(s) needed, PGP trust model
gpg: depth: 0 valid:   1 signed:   0 trust: 0 -, 0q, 0n, 0m, 0f, 1u
gpg: next trustdb check due at 2013 -02-11
gpg: Total number processed: 1
gpg:          new signatures: 1
```

"That's a quick rundown of working with keyservers; we may sometimes post our keys to a keyserver for convenience--we could even send messages in the name, e-mail or comment section of a public key we use to sign another key. The *key* thing to remember-- no pun intended, eh Bob? The key thing to remember about keyservers is that once you put a key up there, it's very difficult to delete, and it very quickly gets propagated to other keyservers all over the world."

Bob asks, "So, how important is it that I know how to use keyservers?"

"At first, don't worry too much about it. Look on the other side of that page I just gave you, there's some listed there," says Sam, as Bob looks at the sheet:

Server Name	Notes
keys.gnupg.net	This is an alias for the official SKS pool (see next entry). You can see a list of IP addresses for servers currently in the pool with the command "host keys. gnupg.net."
pool.sks-keyservers.net	The main pool of SKS keyservers. Each pooled keyserver synchronizes with other servers, so it is only necessary to submit changes once to update the entire OpenPGP network. See http://www.sks-keyservers.net for more information about SKS pools.
keyserver.pgp.com	PGP Global Directory; a "verified" keyserver, meaning key holders sending keys must verify their e-mail addresses by responding to an e-mail before the key is published.
pgp.mit.edu	MIT Public Key Server. **Do not use this keyserver**. The OpenPGP community recommends against using it because the server does not reliably synchronize with other servers.

Sam accepts a plate of tiramisu from the flight attendant and says, "Bob, let's take a break here, and have some of this delicious dessert!"

"Yes," replies Bob, "after cake, you can explain to me about key revocation."

"Key revocation, coming right up--but before that, a quick general overview on how to edit a key," says Sam.

6.3 REVIEW QUESTIONS

1. Why would you want to upload your key to a public keyserver?
2. Why would you *not* want to upload your key to a public keyserver?
3. How likely do you think it is that two public keys would have the same key ID? The same fingerprint?
4. Does Bob seem more relaxed? Why might that be?

CHAPTER 7

Editing and Revoking a Public Key

"Why would I want to edit my key? What is there to edit? And what about revoking a key?" asks Bob. "You had a lot to say about key revocation earlier, but I still don't really understand what that means, and how it works. Can you explain?"

Sam responds: "Your public key pair is more than just the raw bits of the public and private keys used for encrypting and digital signing. There are other pieces of data that get bound up with your key pair: the name and e-mail address you enter when you generate the key, the time/date the key was created, the time/date the key expires, even the passphrase you use to protect the key."

"Some of those things cannot be changed, obviously, like the time/date the key was created; some can be changed but probably shouldn't until you're more experienced with GnuPG, like name and e-mail address; and there are some things where it makes a certain amount of sense to know how to change them, like the passphrase protecting the key, signing someone else's key, setting an expiration date or revoking a key entirely," Sam explains. "So it's good to know how to edit a key."

7.1 EDITING KEYS

"There are a lot of ways to edit keys: for example, there are four different ways to sign a key[1], and there's a way you can direct others to a particular keyserver to retrieve your key[2]. All key editing starts with the basic GnuPG --edit-key command. The syntax is like this":

```
gpg --edit-key user-id [commands]
```

---

[1]They are `sign` (make a signature on the key), `lsign` (sign for local purposes but never export the signature), `nrsign` (sign nonrevocably, meaning the signature cannot be revoked) and `tsign` (make a "trust" signature, similar to the --edit-key `trust` command but used within groups rather than globally). These special types of signature can be combined (e.g., a key can be signed nonrevocably, for local use only).

[2]The command --edit-key `keyID` keyserver will prompt for a URL of the preferred keyserver to refresh the key from, when needed. This is a preference that users may override.

"You have to specify which key to edit, whether it's by the user ID, name, or e-mail address. GnuPG returns an error message with command syntax summary if you don't specify a user. You can also include a command (e.g., `passwd` to change a passphrase), otherwise GnuPG returns a special key-editing command prompt after it lists some key information." Sam says, nodding at the screen. "Like this":

```
$ gpg --edit-key 1A0F711A
gpg (GnuPG/MacGPG2) 2.0.18; Copyright (C) 2011 Free Software Foundation, Inc.
This is free software: you are free to change and redistribute it.
There is NO WARRANTY, to the extent permitted by law.

Secret key is available.
pub  2048R/1A0F711A  created: 2013-01-15  expires: 2015-07-04  usage: SC
                     trust: ultimate      validity: ultimate
sub  2048R/DDBB6A4D  created: 2013-01-15  expires: 2015-07-04  usage: E
[ultimate] (1). Sam Mallory <sam.mallory.404@gmail.com>
gpg> help
```

"With the command `gpg --edit-key 1A0F711A`, I tell GnuPG I want to edit my key. GnuPG tells me about the key (so I can make sure it's the one I want to edit), and gives me this new prompt, `gpg >`. If I type the word 'help' here, GnuPG lists a few dozen key-editing commands." Sam pauses and says, "But I won't do that. I just wanted to show you how it works, so you know how to change a key expiration date[3] or revoke a signature on someone's key[4]. Also, you need to save changes before you exit this key-editing mode[5]."

"As long as you read the prompts, you should be OK. Also, you exit from the `gpg >` prompt by typing `quit` and hitting Enter; if you've made changes, GnuPG prompts you to save them before quitting. Next, we'll revoke a key," says Sam.

---

[3]Enter the command `gpg --edit-key key-id expire` and you'll be prompted for a new expiration date for `key-id` (see Chapter 3).

[4]Enter the command `gpg --edit-key key-id revsig` and you'll be prompted regarding which signatures to revoke. Novices should use this with caution, if at all.

[5]After entering change information, at the `gpg >` prompt enter `save` and GnuPG saves the change(s) and exits to the OS command line. Enter `quit` and, if you've made changes that haven't been saved, GnuPG may prompt you to save before exiting.

7.2 REVOKING A KEY

"You've got to be able to revoke any key you've created, especially if it doesn't have an expiration date[6]." Sam says, glancing at Bob for confirmation.

"If you're revoking a key by choice, you have the advantage of being able to plan how you do it. So if you are changing jobs or want to migrate to a stronger key, give a warning to the people who use it. More importantly, when you generate your new key, *sign it with your old key* before you revoke the old key. That makes it easier for your associates to accept your new key as *yours* and not an attempt by someone else to steal your identity." Sam goes on: "But if your key *has* been compromised, issue the revocation immediately and notify your associates: you may need to distribute your new key in person, as we've already discussed."

"But Sam, please explain how I revoke a key? You talk about revoking, and you talk about a revocation certificate--how does it all work?" asks Bob.

7.2.1 The Revocation Process

"Ideally," begins Sam, "when you create a new key you also generate a *revocation certificate* for it. This 'certificate' is basically a signed message from yourself (the keyholder) announcing your key is invalid and should not be used. You store this certificate somewhere safe--a safe deposit box or anywhere it won't be easily found or associated with the computer you use with that public key. If you lose control over your key (someone stole your computer or cracked your passphrase), you can use the revocation certificate to revoke the key."

"So there are two steps in revoking a key: generating the certificate and keeping it safe, and publishing the certificate when you need to revoke the key." Sam, seeing Bob is still looking confused, says, "I'll show you."

7.2.2 Creating the Revocation Certificate

"The command to generate a revocation certificate is this":

```
gpg --gen-revoke key-id
```

[6]See Chapter 3.

"Doing it this way, the certificate is echoed to the screen (GnuPG produces this output using ASCII-armoring), or you can use the `--output` option to specify a file in which the certificate is saved. Here's what it looks like," Sam says as he enters the command:

```
$ gpg --gen-revoke 1A0F711A
sec  2048R/1A0F711A 2013-01-15 Sam Mallory <sam.mallory.404@gmail.com>
Create a revocation certificate for this key? (y/N) y
```

"I've entered my own key ID, and GnuPG returns information about the key: it's a secret key, 2048 bits, the date I created it and my name and e-mail," says Sam.

"Do I have to use the key ID?" asks Bob, "What about name or e-mail?"

Sam answers, "Yes, you could use those, but it's better to get the key ID, in case you have more than one key with the same name or e-mail; the key ID is unique."

"If it's the correct key, answer yes to the first prompt, and then indicate why you're revoking the key. I prefer not to advertise that I've had my key compromised--it reflects poorly on my security habits--so I'd just say the key has been superseded or is no longer used, or perhaps not specify any reason at all":

```
Please select the reason for the revocation:
  0 = No reason specified
  1 = Key has been compromised
  2 = Key is superseded
  3 = Key is no longer used
  Q = Cancel
(Probably you want to select 1 here)
Your decision? 0
```

"The next prompt is for a 'description'; again, my inclination is to not give away too much information, though you can enter a general message ('Contact me for details') or anything you like--or nothing," Sam says as he continues typing:

```
Enter an optional description; end it with an empty line:
> Contact me for details
>
Reason for revocation: No reason specified
original revocation certificate
Is this okay? (y/N) y
```

"Next, enter the passphrase for that key. Without the passphrase, you can't do anything--another reason to generate the revocation certificate right away after generating the key, so if you *do* forget the key, at least you can revoke it." Sam enters his passphrase and GnuPG returns a message along with the certificate:

```
You need a passphrase to unlock the secret key for
user: "Sam Mallory <sam.mallory.404@gmail.com>"
2048-bit RSA key, ID 1A0F711A, created 2013-01-15

ASCII armored output forced.
Revocation certificate created.

Please move it to a medium which you can hide away; if Mallory gets
access to this certificate he can use it to make your key unusable.
It is smart to print this certificate and store it away, just in case
your media become unreadable.  But have some caution:  The print system of
your machine might store the data and make it available to others!
-----BEGIN PGP PUBLIC KEY BLOCK-----
Comment: A revocation certificate should follow

iQE+BCABAgAoBQJRGQ4ZIR0Ab3JpZ2luYWwgcmV2b2NhdGlvbiBjZXJ0aWZpY2F0
ZQAKCRA7O7OzGg9xGtUUCACLb4o25Wh7g0gdeVnGNjaFRaubkV0Pnj2FqU/BIk3d
F81YI1YvMqb3OHGn5bVR58XXEiTgGg46CKmXorPeiPdysCqCV3sI6cGvLwvXcvdP
OfntHK1HVXqZdC+4kWIUHnMfOM4Z9G2yYcCzOlioDw00ZXSsh6jRmG5epfjWuBuJ
I0TmMingZ8hXJmD9TOivuXTf/yIeuntJ03K9ncQ2+zPULsF83PnQEsUPXei188Zn
QQgs0IpFuRaEcu3ea8bzjLXQXt1A9x4wZ36TS5rDB5GtTX717dGstuxby7oNVOmv
6a+/gU0Fjp95LO+WDrO8mxE8UMxUCPzEcRmFv95H5ZrI
=jSpX
-----END PGP PUBLIC KEY BLOCK-----
```

Sam explains, "That PGP block is the revocation certificate; I can cut and paste that block to use it, but it's easier (if I'm careful) to send the output directly to a file. I'd use this command to save the revocation certificate to `revkey.asc`":

```
gpg --output revkey.asc --gen-revoke key-id
```

Bob scans the GnuPG message above the PGP block and asks, pointedly, "Why does it say that about Mallory accessing the certificate, is that bad for you?"

"Oh, that's just a coincidence: 'Mallory' is a name used in the 'cryptographic cast of characters'. It's a name--like Bob or Alice or Eve--that stands in for a role. It's a placeholder, and just a coincidence, the same as we use the names 'Bob' and 'Alice' when talking about two people communicating with each other. Also, 'Eve' is an eavesdropper, and 'Mallory' (or 'Mallet', sometimes) is a 'malicious attacker'. Nothing at all like myself, of course."

"I see," says Bob, "of course. But as we've already determined that you are using a pseudonym, it was an interesting choice on your part, no? Please, do continue."

Sam, flustered, says, "Yes, where were we? Oh yes, revoking the key."

7.2.3 Revoking a Key

"There are two steps to issuing the revocation: first, revoke the key on your own keyring--when you are ready to stop using--and second, publish the revocation to a public keyserver, if you've published it to a keyserver," Sam explains, "So, first, load the certificate into your keyring like this":

```
$ gpg --import revkey.asc
```

"Once I import the revocation certificate I can no longer use the key to sign anything but I can still decrypt any ciphertexts encrypted with it." explains Sam. "Next, I publish the revocation to any keyservers I posted my key to, like this":

```
$ gpg --send-keys 1A0F711A
gpg: sending key 1A0F711A to hkp server keys.gnupg.net
```

"And that's all; if you want to see that your revocation was accepted by the keyserver, you'll have to go check the keyserver directly and look up the key ID."

Sam adds, "And don't forget, if you're doing a routine revocation, use the old key to sign your new key *before* you revoke the old one. That way your associates can trust the new key without too much trouble if they refresh their keyrings from a keyserver periodically. Just be sure to warn them the key is changing."

"Is this the only way to revoke a key, Sam?" asks Bob.

7.2.4 A Different Way to Revoke

"If you don't want to generate a revocation certificate, you can use the --edit-key command--as long as you've got your key passphrase," answers Sam. "You still need to update a keyserver to publish the revocation. Here's how":

```
$ gpg --edit-key 528BE85B revkey
gpg (GnuPG/MacGPG2) 2.0.18; Copyright (C) 2011 Free Software Foundation, Inc.
This is free software: you are free to change and redistribute it.
There is NO WARRANTY, to the extent permitted by law.

Secret key is available.

pub  2048R/528BE85B  created: 2013-02-11  expires: 2013-02-16  usage: SC
                     trust: ultimate      validity: ultimate
sub  2048R/85BCE1A0  created: 2013-02-11  expires: 2013-02-16  usage: E
[ultimate] (1). Chester A. Arthur <chet@example.net>

Do you really want to revoke the entire key? (y/N) y
```

"From this point, it's almost exactly the same process as before; the big difference is that when you're finished, you go back to the gpg> prompt. From there, quit and you're prompted to save changes. Then, publish the revocation to a keyserver, same as before," finishes Sam.

"Thank you, Sam, everything is very clear," replies Bob, "or should I call you Mallet?" Bob pauses just a moment and then says, "It seems as though we've covered most of my questions about GnuPG, but I'm sure there must be more I should know about. Do you mind if I check my e-mail and take some notes, that should take about half an hour--maybe we can wrap things up then?"

"Sure, Bob," says Sam, "that's fine."

7.3 COMMAND SUMMARY AND REVIEW

Command	Description and Notes
gpg --edit-key *user-id*[commands]	Edit key identified by *user-id* (name or e-mail is also allowed); commands are optional, if left out, GnuPG prompts for interactive editing.
gpg --gen-revoke *key-id*	Generate a revocation certificate for *key-id* (user ID, name or e-mail). Resulting certificate will be echoed to the screen; use --output option to output to a file.
gpg -o *revkey.asc* --gen-revoke *key-id*	Generate revocation certificate for *key-id* and save as *revkey.asc*.
gpg --import *revkey.asc*	Import the revocation certificate (*revkey.asc*) and revoke the key locally.
gpg --keyserver *keyserver* --send-keys *key-id*	Publish revocation to *keyserver*.
gpg --edit-key *user-id* revkey	Revoke a key using the GnuPG key editor.

7.4 REVIEW QUESTIONS

1. Who are some of the other "players" in the cryptographic cast of characters? (Hint: use your favorite search engine for more information.) Why is it helpful to use these *placeholder names*?
2. If you lost your passphrase for an old key that's been published on a keyserver, is there anything you can do about it? (Hint: you can't revoke that key, but you can sign it with some other key--remember that keys can have comments.)
3. Change the expiration date on your public key. How would you add (or edit) the user name with --edit-key? How? (hint: it's not obvious or easy.)
4. What's the difference between revoking a key and disabling a key?

CHAPTER 8

Security Practices and Tips

Bob spends the next half hour or so sipping coffee and jotting notes on what he's learned so far, and, like Sam, generally doing business-related busy work.

"Sam, I have just received a message from my wife," Bob announces, "You will be interested to hear what she says":

Dear Bobby, how glad I am to hear from you, and that you have successfully boarded your plane--you must be enjoying the first class treatment! You know how worried I get when I do not hear from you when I expect to--but I am always keeping my eyes on you. And of course, Walter and I will meet your flight. We are both looking forward to meeting this new friend of yours...

Bob trails off, and Sam presses him to continue. "Oh, that's about all she wrote," stammers Bob, "Just, you know, 'love and kisses, Eve', more or less," but Bob reads on, realizing that Sam has control over his network connection and therefore can see the entire message himself. "She wrote":

...this new friend of yours.
I missed my snookum-wookums so much. Love and kisses.
Eve

"Yes, that's delightful," says Sam as he cringes inwardly, "I, too, look forward to meeting your lovely wife and cat. You had more questions about encryption?"

"Actually, yes I do," says Bob, "a few. First, please explain how I make sure a software file I download is properly verified?"

8.1 VERIFYING SOFTWARE DOWNLOADS

"One common attack is to trick you into installing malicious software that gives the attacker control over your system. One way to do that is tricking you into thinking it is software that you really want," Sam begins.

"Oh, like GnuPG? I downloaded it while you were monitoring my network activities in the United States. Have I downloaded a malicious version that you created just for me? One that keeps track of everything I do on my computer?" asks Bob.

"Well, uh, no, of course we would never do something like that to you, Bob, but maybe the SSS has a version that monitors all your secrets," says Sam. "So, to be sure you have the right version of GnuPG, you must verify the signature file for the download."

Bob asks, "OK, I downloaded GnuPG and installed it--but how can I be sure that version of GnuPG hasn't been hacked and delivered to me by an attacker instead of the real program? I can't very well verify the signature of the hacked software *with* the hacked software--that can't be right." Bob looks directly at Sam.

"That's right, I mean, not right. You should *never* use software you download to verify itself." Sam seems to be getting a bit uncomfortable as Bob continues: "I think that one way to verify this software is to try downloading it from other sites and compare all the downloads; if they are all the same, then maybe it's OK."

Sam brightens visibly and says, "Yes, exactly! Just download the software, with the signature file and signing keys from a couple of different mirrors and compare with what you've got--that should work!"

Bob's not buying it though, "That's what I thought, but if my attacker--I will call him 'Mallory', like GnuPG says--Mallory sees my network activity, and if she can replace a download once, then I think she can also replace the download two or three or fifty times, and every time it will look the same."

Sam says nothing as Bob continues: "So I asked Alice--a lovely young woman, and very bright. Also my wife's niece, did you know that?" Bob goes on, "I asked Alice if she would get me a copy of GnuPG, she gave me the Liveboot version of Ubuntu Linux, which I ran from my DVD drive, and I discovered that the version of GnuPG I downloaded was different from the one she gave me--which she verified. I decided to trust Alice, so I've been using her version."

Sam continues to say nothing as Bob continues: "I checked the signing keys on public keyservers and verified that the signature on the code Alice gave me was correct, and that the signatures on the files I downloaded from Mallory are not correct." Bob pauses, then says, "I think GnuPG worked quite well for me."

8.1.1 Verifying a Download With a Hash Value
Sam says, "Um. That's great, Bob. You know if you don't have a copy of GnuPG that you trust, you can do a hash of the download and compare that to the good hash value published online?"

"Yes, I discovered I can get the SHA256 checksum value from the download site, and can run a program on my system to calculate the SHA256 checksum of the file I downloaded. But I haven't been able to figure out how to do that part, can you explain how that works, Sam?"

Sam, glad to change the topic, answers, "SHA256 is a 256-bit secure hash algorithm. That means it's considered a cryptographically secure way to generate a unique 256-bit value for any given file. When a software developer publishes a download file, they calculate the hash for the file and publish it as well. When you download the file, you calculate the hash on your download and compare it to the published hash. If they match, you can be confident the two files are identical."

"The hash itself doesn't give any information about the owner or publisher of the file (like a digital signature does) but it will give an indication of whether the file you download is the same as the file originally published online." Sam finishes.

8.1.2 Calculating a Hash Value on Different OSes
"It's easiest to calculate the hash value on a file with Linux," says Sam. "Here's the command":

```
sha256sum filename
```

"`sha256sum` is a command that comes with Linux; there are options you can use, but for checking a hash, this will work":

```
$ sha256sum gnupg-2.0.19.tar
efa23a8a925adb51c7d3b708c25b6d000300f5ce37de9bdec6453be7b419c622 gnupg-2.0.19.tar
```

"Compare that result to the value published with the download." Sam says. "It's about the same on Windows, except the command is named `sha256sum.exe`. On OS X, the command is `shasum`":

```
$ $ shasum tails-i386-0.16.iso
e4ba85b1e598b80c7633e7ece19d264e39fac879 tails-i386-0.16.iso
```

"Verifying the hash value is good, but not always good enough, especially if you are comparing to a hash value supplied directly with the download--you need to be confident that the hash value you're comparing is trustworthy." Sam continues, "It's best to use a signature and signing keys."

"Yes," says Bob, "that's what I thought. By the way, Sam, how much do you know about my country?"

"Well, ah, that's an interesting question," begins Sam, but Bob cuts him off: "Yes, before you answer, I know you claim to be a spy with dealings in my country, but I think you know very little about Sylvania. You did not recognize the name of our leader. I think you may have other gaps in your knowledge. You are aware of our leader's policy against publishing dissent or criticism of regime?"

"Yes, of course, it's horrible--you must be horribly repressed in your country…" begins Sam, but Bob cuts him off:

"Actually, it is not *so* horrible in my homeland. In many ways, yes, Sylvania is backward, yet we have great regard for traditions of great democracies like your United States. But Chairman Bob is old-fashioned, and when he came to power in 1936, he took on the trappings of a dictator. It was the fashion, as you know."

Sam, boggling at the revelation that the Sylvanian Leader has been ruling for over 75 years, opens his mouth to ask and is cut off again by Bob, "Yes, Leader is 124 years old this year, but this is not unusual in our nation: something to do with our yoghurt, I am told. However," he continues, "while it is treason to print criticism, dissent is encouraged as long as it is *not* in print. Anyone may say anything they like, and artistic representations are encouraged: music, paintings, even theater."

"You may well ask why this is so: our Chairman is popular because he rules in accordance with wishes of citizens--citizens present their cases and achieve consensus in the marketplace of ideas, and then

Chairman Bob announces the laws and rulings that best meet the needs of Sylvania's citizens."

Sam, amazed, asks, "But your Internet access is filtered--what about freedom of surfing? Don't you want to be able to go to any web site you like?"

Bob says, "In Sylvania, Internet access is supported for furthering the arts, science, and commerce in Sylvania. Bandwidth in my country, like petroleum, is a limited resource, so we try not to waste it on memes and pictures of cats."

"Sam, life in Sylvania is not so bad: we have our freedoms, even if it doesn't seem that way at first glance. Our culture is different from yours, but we believe as you do in the rights of all. You will see when we arrive."

Bob, pausing to sip some coffee, adds, "Also, you should know that citizens who criticize Sylvanian system or Sylvanian leaders are not actually executed: the usual punishment for a first offense is a 10-year term as support staff in the Sylvanian Legislature. It is punitive--Sylvanian legislators are very bad bosses--but not excessively so. Let's get back to talking about keeping secrets, please."

"Sam, you've mentioned several times to use strong passphrases, can you explain what you mean by that?"

8.2 PASSPHRASES: DOING THEM RIGHT

Sam says, "Conventional wisdom insists that 'strong' passphrases have at least eight characters and include upper- and lowercase letters, numerals, and special characters. The idea is to defend against password cracking, and particularly against brute-force attacks: if a password is a name followed by a number, it can be discovered fairly quickly with a brute-force attack; short passwords with just six characters, even if they include numerals and symbols, are also easily cracked."

"The math is easy: with 95 characters available for passphrases[1] we have exactly 95 one-character passphrases ('E' or '?', for example), so you could brute force a one-character passphrase by hand, by trying every letter, number and character. If you are very lucky, that attack could succeed in one try; if you are very unlucky, it would take the

[1]Includes 26 uppercase and 26 lowercase letters, 10 numerals, and 33 characters.

maximum of 95 tries; on average you'd succeed after trying about half of all possible combinations. If it takes 1 second to try each single-character passphrase, you'd need between 1 and 95 seconds to crack it, but on average you can expect to spend about 43 seconds."

Sam continues: "For a 2-character passphrase, there are 95 options for the first character, and each of those options can be coupled with 95 options for the second character. Total number of combinations is $95 \times 95 = 9025$. Now, a brute-force attack will succeed in about an hour and a quarter instead of under a minute."

"Each character you add to the passphrase multiplies the total number of possible passphrases by 95, so a 10-character passphrase has 95 raised to the tenth power. That's $95 \times 95 \times 95 \times 95 \times 95 \times 95 \times 95 \times 95 \times 95 \times 95$, about 60,000,000,000,000,000,000 different combinations. That's *60 billion billion.*"

"If you used a lower-case-only passphrase, you'd have far fewer possible combinations: it would be 26 (number of lowercase letters) raised to the tenth power: 26^{10}. That comes to about 147,000,000,000,000, or about 147,000 billion, a tiny fraction (about 1/400,000th) of the possibilities when you use upper- and lowercase letters, numerals and symbols."

"So, 10-character passphrases should be safe, then, no?" Bob asks.

"Oh, goodness no," replies Sam. "Well, not necessarily, anyway. It depends on who wants to crack your password, and how many computers they have at their disposal, as well as whether your password is 'easy' to guess (by that, I mean, using '123456password', or any passphrase that might be on a list of easy-to-guess passphrases). Let's say your passphrase is reasonably random-seeming. With a 10-character lower-case-only passphrase, it takes (on average) about 70,000 billion trials to discover the passphrase. If one computer can try 1,000 passphrases per second (a reasonable supposition), it would take that computer about 70 billion seconds, or a couple of thousand years."

"Is that good for my passphrase?" asks Bob.

"Not really. If it takes one computer two or three thousand years, you can crack the passphrase in two or three years with 1,000 computers. That drops to a week or so with 10,000 computers--a couple of hours with a million computers. If one computer costs $100--that cheap, because you're buying in bulk, plus you don't need individual disk drives, video display cards, and so on--that means you can crack almost any 10-character (lower-case-only) passphrase in an hour or two, for just $100 million," says Sam.

"That seems like a lot of money, so I shouldn't worry too much, right?" asks Bob, but Sam says, "We're talking about multinational corporations and government agencies--with those guys, $100 million is a rounding error, it's petty cash. The Pentagon spends about that much on one F-35 fighter jet."

"It could still take years to brute force a strong 10-character pass-phrase (with upper- and lowercase letters, numerals, and symbols), but the people who write password cracking software rely on users picking passphrases with some pattern in them, like names followed by num-bers, so they focus attacks on likely combinations rather than simply trying every passphrase from 'A' to 'zzzzzzzzzz'."

"If you use a 12-character passphrase without patterns, you should be safe--from brute-force passphrase cracking. You still have to defend against keylogging and network monitoring and spoofing and *social engineering*[2] and *rubber-hose cryptanalysis*[3] and all the other strategies for defeating your passphrase." Sam pauses, but starts quickly before Bob can ask his next question:

"That's not all, Bob. Remembering 12 random-seeming characters is difficult, and with GnuPG, if you forget your public key passphrase, you've lost the ability to use that passphrase completely. No passphrase recovery (other than trying to use passphrase cracking software yourself). So, most users wind up writing their passphrases down, or even using pass-phrase keeper software[4]. In many cases, cracking passphrases is as easy as looking for yellow-stickies on, around, or under the computer itself."

"Is there nothing to be done?" Bob asks. "Why use passphrases at all then?"

---

[2]Social engineering: use of interpersonal interactions to convince a person to reveal a passphrase or take some action against their own interest.
[3]Rubber-hose cryptanalysis: use of torture or coercion to recover a passphrase.
[4]Bruce Schneier's Password Safe (http://pwsafe.org/) works on Windows, numerous "related pro-jects" support other platforms (http://pwsafe.org/relatedprojects.shtml).

"You can use a passphrase 'safe', but you've got to have a very strong passphrase to access the safe, and even then, just having it could be an invitation to enhanced interrogation." Sam continues: "A more secure option is to use a sentence or verse or phrase that you can easily remember (but hard to guess), and build a passphrase from the first letter (or two or three) of each word, using punctuation and numerals where appropriate[5]. For example: 'Mary had a little lamb, its fleece was white as snow. And everywhere that Mary went, that lamb was sure to go.' can be turned into a passphrase like this":

```
Mhall,ifwwas.AetMw,tlws2g.
```

"Notice how I used punctuation and the numeral 2 (instead of the 't' from the word 'to'); both make the passphrase harder to guess. That's a 26-character passphrase, but easy to remember. I wouldn't use that one because it's obvious, but you could use some other phrase or verse that you're likely to know and remember but that an attacker would not know about. According to some experts, passphrases have outlived their usefulness, and should be supplemented with a second form of authentication[6]. For now, a good passphrase is fine, just keep it safe."

Bob ponders a bit, and then asks, "You also mentioned about RAMs and caches, how do they expose my passphrases or plaintexts? Explain please."

8.3 DANGERS OF RAM CACHE AND OTHER SYSTEM ARTIFACTS

"Your computer changes its 'state'--contents of its working memory, or RAM, as well as contents of its hard drives--whenever you do anything with it. A program may create a temporary file to keep track of what files you have open, or maintain a log of every song and video you play. Web browsers notoriously store all kinds of history files and logs on everything you do online. Your browser may expose all kinds of information, including all personal information, credit card numbers, and web site passphrases." says Sam.

---

[5]For example, see "Strong passphrases and password cracking" (http://crypto.loshin.com/2013/02/01/strong-passphrases-and-password-cracking/), also "Password Tips" from Purdue University's SecurePurdue web site (http://www.purdue.edu/securePurdue/bestpractices/passtips.cfm).
[6]"Two-factor authentication" (http://crypto.loshin.com/2013/02/01/two-factor-authentication/).

"So maybe I should encrypt my entire computer?" asks Bob.

"Yes, actually, you should; that's my next topic. You should encrypt your hard drives, but there's more to it than that. Even programs that don't write files with sensitive information may still store sensitive data (like your passphrases) in the computer's working memory--the RAM. When you power down your computer, whatever is in RAM eventually dissolves away[7]. And powering off means powering everything off, no hibernation or sleep mode: those store system state-- the contents of RAM--making it easier for an attacker to subvert your system."

"Remember, even though passphrases and plaintexts may not be written to files, they can still be vulnerable while your computer is turned on because that data is in RAM." Sam adds, "You should also be careful with your command history when you're using GnuPG at the command line."

"The command line history can trip you up, since it documents your computer activities. In the Windows command prompt, pressing F7 displays command history, but only for the current session. When you close the command prompt window in Windows, that history disappears, but things are different in Linux and OS X, in both good and bad ways. Good because your history is saved (so you can more easily browse through old commands) and the default number of commands is pretty high[8], but that can be bad, since saving your history means saving evidence of your activities."

"The thing to do, if you're worried about leaving evidence behind, is to remove it: On Windows, that's as easy as closing the command prompt window, but on OS X and Linux, you can clear the history with the command `history -c`, but also securely delete the history file itself (`.bash_history`, found in the GnuPG home directory[9]; note the filename starts with a period) containing the history[10]."

---

[7]On some systems, data in RAM can persist for minutes, even longer when the system is cooled before powering off. See "Lest We Remember: Cold Boot Attacks on Encryption Keys" (https://citp.princeton.edu/research/memory/).

[8]The default for OS X is 500 commands and for Linux, 1,000.

[9]Use the command `gpg --help` to find the GnuPG home directory.

[10]For more, see "Managing shell command history in OS X/Linux" (http://crypto.loshin.com/2013/02/13/managing-shell-command-history-in-os-xlinux/).

Sam continues: "Another thing that happens is that GnuPG, through the Pinentry program, takes your passphrase and holds it in memory (the RAM) to unlock access to your key. By default, GnuPG waits for 10 minutes before erasing your passphrase from RAM. That way you can decrypt or sign more than once without having to re-enter the passphrase."

"If you're really nervous, you can change the configuration to reduce the *time to live* for the cached passphrase, or even turn caching off entirely by setting the time-to-live value to zero." Sam thinks, and says, "If you're using OS X, one thing you really *shouldn't* do is to click on the 'Save in Keychain' box when Pinentry opens up and you enter your passphrase. If you do, you can lose control of your public key entirely--because your passphrase is now only protected by the strength of your system passphrase. And you might not even realize you're doing it. I've done it. It's bad enough that the system doesn't forget your passphrase, but when you actively ask the system to save it for you then you're in trouble."

Sam adds, "The system holds onto your cached passphrase for 10 minutes (the default) even if you close the terminal window. So be careful: it's one of those things that make me believe Linux is a better choice than OS X or Windows for doing anything related to security."

"Thanks Sam," says Bob, "that's helpful. But what about encrypting my hard drive? Is your hard drive encrypted?"

"Oh yes," answers Sam, "mine is definitely encrypted. It's pretty easy, too; you can get the step-by-step details online, it's different on Windows, OS X, and Linux, but not too hard. It is definitely worth doing, though."

8.4 FULL DISK ENCRYPTION

"Broad strokes here: doing full disk encryption (FDE) means that your entire hard drive is encrypted. If you take the hard drive out and put it on another system, or if you boot from a rescue disc, all you'll see is ciphertext." Sam pauses expectantly, so Bob asks, "If it's all encrypted, how can I use any of the data on it? Do I have to decrypt it all every time I log in?"

"Great question!" Sam replies. "When you log back in to a system with FDE, there's a little program that encrypts any data being written to the disk and that decrypts any data that is being read from the disk. It's very efficient, so it doesn't really affect system performance. If you log in with the right passphrase, that program will work; if you don't have the passphrase, you won't be able to read any data from that disk."

"But Sam, in that case, when I'm using the computer, it's as if the disk *isn't* encrypted and all of my system is an open book," asks Bob, uncertainly adding, "Isn't it?"

"Exactly," answers Sam. "That's why you should never leave your computer turned on when you're not using it, or when it's out of your control. And also why you should keep your computer off any networks, and also don't let anyone plug in to your USB ports. Because there are forensic software programs, sometimes used by law enforcement agencies, that can copy the contents of your RAM, or your entire hard drive."

"Well, then why bother encrypting my hard drive at all, Sam?" Bob asks.

8.4.1 How Good Is FDE?

"FDE is an excellent security practice, *as long as you are aware of the weaknesses*," Sam says. "Because as long as you are vigilant, and keep the system powered down when you don't have control over it, you'll be pretty safe."

"Thank you, Sam, that explains what Walter was doing earlier, while you were in the washroom." Bob turns to face a burly gentleman standing at the entry to the first class compartment and says, "Walter, allow me to introduce you to my new friend, Mallory." Turning back to Sam, Bob says, "Mallory, this is Walter, one very cool cat who works for my wife. I should have known that he would be on this flight; he watches over us, particularly when we may need some protection."

Sam begins to panic, glancing back and forth, at Bob and then at Walter. "When you went to the washroom, I discovered Walter in coach and explained that you were trying to convince me to betray my nation. The first thing he did was to plug into your notebook and did some fooling around, I don't know what, exactly, but I think now that you have been p0wned--is that the right word, Walter?"

As Walter nods somberly, Bob continues: "So, Sam, rather than I working for you, it is you who will be working for my wife. Chin up, though, it is not so bad to live in Sylvania: you will be given an entry-level job, something honorable yet not too pleasant, perhaps school lunch server or maybe plumber's helper. And in the evenings you will be called upon to help train members of our security service."

"In any case," continues Bob, "Please explain how effective FDE is; you can be sure I will not leave my system turned on when it is unattended. But take your time, and have a beverage if you need a moment to collect your wits, by all means."

Walter removes Sam's computer from his tray table, replacing it with a tumbler of scotch, and as Bob plays Scramble with Friends[11] Sam attempts to regain enough composure to answer Bob's question.

Sam begins: "When used correctly, FDE can be extremely resistant even to efforts by the government.[12] I mean, the US government, but I guess any other government will have the same problem. The two big things to remember are keep the computer turned off when unattended and use a strong passphrase."

Bob interrupts: "Yes, that's funny, as Walter told me your FDE passphrase was 'password123'. I think that is not a strong passphrase, do you agree?"

"Well, no, unh, I guess it's not too strong, Bob," mutters Sam.

Bob touches Sam's wrist and says, "Well, never mind. Everything will be fine for you, don't worry, you'll see. But before you return to Walter's seat in coach, tell me how to do FDE."

"Aw, heck, Bob, here's a FAQ I wrote," Sam says, handing a sheet of paper to Bob. "I'm coming Walter, where were you sitting?"

---

[11]Scramble with Friends is a popular time killer often played on a smartphone while sitting on an airplane. It has nothing to do with encryption.
[12]See "Efficacy of full disk encryption" http://crypto.loshin.com/2012/11/19/efficacy-of-full-disk-encryption/.

"Oh, a very nice seat, just across from the toilet, all the way back. There are only two babies in the seats behind, and you have the honor of sitting between two of Sylvania's most popular wrestlers."

Bob says, "See you later, Mallory," as he turns to peruse Sam's FAQ:

8.5 ENCRYPTING YOUR SYSTEM HARD DRIVE FAQ

Encrypting the disk can be done with encryption programs included with Windows and OS X, or with the TrueCrypt program on Windows, OS X, or Linux. Not all Windows editions include the Microsoft BitLocker program; if your system does not, you can still encrypt the disk with TrueCrypt.

8.5.1 How it Works

The process begins by starting the FDE encryption program of choice (FileVault, BitLocker, or TrueCrypt) to encrypt the fixed drive on your computer. It may take hours to actually finish encrypting, though you can continue to work with the system while it is encrypting. When done, everything on your drive will be encrypted and accessible only by the authorized user, when logged in.

The encrypted disk is most secure when turned off. When you must turn it on, you should not permit any connection, either by wi-fi, network cable, or any other hardware connection.

If you're using a cloud service to sync files, all your files on that service are stored in plaintext. If the provider encrypts stored data, that data will most likely be encrypted to keys held by the service provider, which cedes control over your sensitive data to the cloud provider. The same goes for running a backup service, like Apple's Time Machine, on a removable disk. All the data on the backup device will be plaintext.

8.5.2 Enabling FDE

Most people do FDE once: they set it up and let it run. Here are quick summaries of how to do it:

TrueCrypt (all OSes): Download the appropriate program file from www.truecrypt.org (don't forget to download and authenticate the signature). For Windows and OS X, the download is an executable program, run it to begin. Linux users may need to do a bit more research before installation.

BitLocker (Windows): Setup may vary from one version/edition to another, but for example, on Windows 7 Ultimate or Enterprise editions, BitLocker can be turned on by entering the Control Panel application, choosing **Security**, clicking on **BitLocker Drive Encryption**, choose a drive to encrypt and follow instructions to enable drive encryption.

FileVault (OS X): Open the System Preferences application; choose Security & Privacy (from the top row). Choose the FileVault panel and follow instructions to activate FDE.

Things to be aware of:

Passphrase: use a strong one, as it is the only thing standing between your private data and an attacker.

Recovery key: if you are offered the option of a recovery key, or any other aid to recovering the encrypted disk, be sure to record it and store the record securely, preferably where only you can access it, and preferably physically removed from where the encrypted system is used.

Restrict physical access to the system while it is in use.

Shut down the system when it is not in use.

8.5.3 About Microsoft BitLocker

BitLocker is proprietary software produced by Microsoft, for Microsoft Windows. In other words, it *should* be the "best solution" for FDE on Windows systems, because it is designed to work only with Windows, and by the same organization that created Windows.

However, Microsoft includes BitLocker in the Enterprise and Ultimate editions of Windows Vista and Windows 7, and in the Pro and Enterprise editions of Windows 8--which means that you may need to upgrade Windows to be able to use BitLocker.

Among the benefits of using BitLocker, particularly for larger organizations, is that encryption recovery can be administered centrally. This is particularly important to maintaining security of data on organizational computers while at the same time retaining access to organizational data assets for authorized users in the organization.

Individuals using consumer editions of Windows will need to upgrade their version of Windows to get access to BitLocker FDE, and may prefer to choose another option to avoid the expense of an upgrade.

8.5.4 About Apple FileVault

As with BitLocker for Windows, users of Apple's OS X will find FileVault to be easy to use and in fact completely transparent to the end user, while at the same time offering organizations mechanisms for authorized users to recover encrypted data.

FileVault is incorporated into the current version of OS X, and can be used on any computer running that OS.

8.5.5 About TrueCrypt

The open source community does not accept the TrueCrypt license as "open." Although it can be downloaded and used for free, and the source code can be reviewed and modified, there are some subtle aspects of the license that make it unacceptable to many free/open source advocates. What this means is that TrueCrypt is not included in any major Linux distributions, but it is still the leading noncommercial solution for FDE on any OS.

Because it is free, popular, and source code available, TrueCrypt should be an adequate solution for users on any platform.

User should be aware that TrueCrypt documentation can be spotty; answers to many questions about installation and configuration may best be found through a well-crafted search query.

After Sam is processed, with extreme thoroughness and three cavity searches, through Sylvanian customs and immigration, Walter escorts the exhausted former spy to a sparsely furnished interview room. Bob and his wife, Eve, are waiting.

"Well, Mr. Mallory," begins Eve, "Do not be overly concerned: your fate is in your own hands, now. You know much about network security, I understand. Should you choose to share your knowledge with us backward Sylvanians, you can earn you great respect and a relatively comfortable lifestyle."

Sam, clearly unhappy, says, "But I have plans here in Sylvania..."

Eve cuts him off, "Yes, Mr. Mallory. There is an old Sylvanian saying, 'Everyone has plans until they get kicked in the...' what is the word in English, Bob? Oh, never mind. You will be allowed to fulfill your obligations here, with Walter assisting you. However, be sure to cooperate fully, or else you may be kicked."

"In the meantime, prepare some notes, as you are expected to lead a seminar for our own agents in advanced topics in encryption and network security next week." Eve, clearly finished with Sam, turns to Walter and commands, "Take him away."

Turning to Bob with an inscrutable smile, Eve says, "Now, my dearest cupcakes, it is time for *you* to cooperate with *me*."

Printed and bound by CPI Group (UK) Ltd, Croydon, CR0 4YY

03/10/2024

01040426-0009